Does Britain Need a Financial Regulator?

Does Britain Need a Financial Regulator?

Statutory Regulation, Private Regulation and Financial Markets

TERRY ARTHUR & PHILIP BOOTH

The Institute of Economic Affairs

First published in Great Britain in 2010 by
The Institute of Economic Affairs
2 Lord North Street
Westminster
London sw1p 3lb
in association with Profile Books Ltd

The mission of the Institute of Economic Affairs is to improve public
understanding of the fundamental institutions of a free society, by analysing
and expounding the role of markets in solving economic and social problems.

A CIP catalogue record for this book is available from the British Library.

ISBN 978 0 255 36593 2

Many IEA publications are translated into languages other than English or
are reprinted. Permission to translate or to reprint should be sought from the
Director General at the address above.

Typeset in Stone by MacGuru Ltd
info@macguru.org.uk

Printed and bound in Great Britain by Hobbs the Printers

CONTENTS

THE AUTHORS

Terry Arthur

Terry Arthur is the IEA Pensions and Financial Regulation Fellow. He was a consulting actuary for most of his career, specialising in institutional investment. He also wrote regularly on pensions, investment and economic issues for several journals. Terry has also held many non-executive directorship positions. Recently he has concentrated more on writing, including the book *Crap: A Guide to Politics*, and regular articles for professional journals and think tanks. He is a regular speaker at educational establishments. Terry is a keen sportsman, winning a rugby blue at Cambridge University in 1962 and playing for England in 1966.

Philip Booth

Philip Booth is Editorial and Programme Director at the Institute of Economic Affairs and Professor of Insurance and Risk Management at the Sir John Cass Business School, City University. He has formerly worked at the Bank of England, advising on financial stability issues – particularly related to the insurance sector. Philip Booth has published widely in the fields of investment and finance, insurance and regulation, social insurance and Catholic social teaching. He is co-author of books on actuarial science and financial mathematics and, among other books, is editor of *Christian Perspectives on the Crash*, *Verdict on the Crash* (published by the IEA) and *The Road to Economic Freedom* – a compilation of work by Nobel Prize winners in economics.

FOREWORD

No recent proposition seems to have been more easily and uncritically accepted than that the recent banking crisis and related widespread disruption in financial markets were the result of the excesses of 'unregulated financial capitalism'. In an era notable for regulatory growth in almost every sphere of economic and social life, it is interesting in itself that the instinctive response of many people to evidence of market discoordination is to assume that regulators must have been insufficiently intrusive. Hayek's 'fatal conceit' that conscious human design must always result in better economic organisation than incremental, decentralised and evolutionary systems is indeed deeply rooted. Market processes, in the popular view, are very likely to descend into chaos unless they are subjected to oversight from powerful regulatory agencies.

It is important to understand what is wrong with the argument that observed dislocations in financial and other markets are caused by too little regulation and can only be overcome by the exercise of greater regulatory power. This paper explains why extensions of state regulation are likely to lead to less rather than more stability and proposes that the powers of the Financial Services Authority (FSA) should not be augmented or its functions redistributed, but rather that in many areas they should simply be abolished. The paper is particularly concerned with investment market regulation and the role of stock exchanges in establishing listing and trading rules.

An important intellectual error that lends support to the increasing powers of regulatory agencies is that of associating all regulatory activity with the state. Governments, according to this way of looking at things, exist to impose constraints and to regulate in the wider social interest, while 'markets' are somehow seen as the antithesis – existing in a realm free of regulatory restraint. This bifurcation has no justification historically, philosophically or in terms of economic theory. Markets are social institutions and can yield the gains to trade only if sufficient trust among the market participants has been established. This trusting environment may be evolved from repeated games of exchange; it may be protected by more formalised rules backed up by the sanction of expulsion or loss of reputation; and, as the complexity and reach of trading relationships become ever more extended, it may require highly developed legal institutions. But these developments are all an integral part of the market mechanism. 'Private governance' is not 'no governance', and the danger of 'state regulation' is that it acts as a very imperfect substitute. In modern conditions a Gresham's Law of regulation seems to apply – bad regulation drives out good.

This observation entirely contradicts the common belief. More than any other proposition it is the assertion that a 'race to the bottom' generally characterises market processes in the absence of a vigilant and benevolent state regulator which lies behind support for ever-increasing oversight. It is forgotten that Gresham's Law itself was a rationalisation of why a 'race to the bottom' might indeed take place when a monopoly state agency tries to enforce parity between coins known by users not to be of equal quality. Left in a competitive environment, however, people have ample incentive to monitor the money they are using and to flee from a debased currency – good money drives out bad. The transition, for example, to a generally less inflationary environment since the late 1970s has been assisted by the abolition of exchange controls and hence greater competition between currencies.

Gresham's Law applied to regulation can be seen operating across the financial sector. In the face of advancing state supervision, the non-profit, cooperative and mutual sectors – so significant to establishing trust in a less heavily regulated era – were undermined. The joint stock company triumphed even in the most hazardous areas of finance where it had once been at a disadvantage – including the provision of stock exchanges. Many mutual institutions converted and became public limited companies while, among those that resisted, the Equitable Life Assurance Society fatefully tried to meet the competition by offering its 'customers' guarantees that eventually proved to be inconsistent with mutual status and destroyed the Society. Savers lost interest in governance and ownership structure – no doubt content in the knowledge that the repository of their trust and their funds was regulated – latterly by the FSA. The argument here is not that the mutual is inherently always a better institutional form for the governance of financial transactions but that the competition between different types of organisation embodying different distributions of control rights and implying different responses to transactional hazards is subtly subverted by state regulation.

We live in a world of information asymmetries and self-interested transactors. State regulation and private governance arrangements have to contend equally with these two basic realities of life. No one denies that adverse selection – the tendency for lower-quality goods and services to be traded and higher-quality ones withdrawn – is a danger if buyers cannot *ex ante* tell the difference between them. But the authors of this Hobart Paper argue persuasively that institutional responses to information and incentive problems, particularly in the area of investment market regulation, can be implemented by private action. Inefficiencies imply large potential gains to individuals and organisations able to respond with innovative solutions, and over time the better responses will tend to displace the poorer ones. The hidden cost of state regulation is that this competitive evolutionary process of experiment and adaptation of governance arrangements within the private sector is distorted and suppressed.

MARTIN RICKETTS

Professor of Economic Organisation
University of Buckingham
Chairman of the Academic Advisory Council of the
Institute of Economic Affairs
July 2010

The views expressed in this monograph are, as in all IEA publications, those of the authors and not those of the Institute (which has no corporate view), its managing trustees, Academic Advisory Council members or senior staff. IEA publications undergo blind peer review. Because this publication was co-authored by a senior member of the IEA staff, the process of peer review was overseen by the chairman of the IEA's Academic Advisory Council.

SUMMARY

- There is a great deal of evidence to suggest that investment markets can develop institutions to regulate themselves. The history of the development of stock exchanges, both in the UK and elsewhere, is testament to that.
- Private forms of regulation, normally through stock exchanges, have led to effective mechanisms to deal with many of the problems that statutory regulation is supposed to deal with. Statutory regulation crowds out the evolution of those mechanisms and replaces the evolution of appropriate investment market regulation with bureaucratic discretion.
- Where statutory regulation has replaced private regulation, there has rarely been an objective rationale or convincing economic explanation.
- The mechanisms of statutory regulation in the UK lack any proper accountability. In effect, they operate outside the rule of law. The FSA has been given very broad objectives, has more or less complete discretion and is not properly accountable to government or Parliament. Indeed, much of the regulatory framework of the FSA is now determined by the European Union.
- The extent of scandals does not seem to have diminished since the advent of statutory regulation.
- Private regulators – through investment exchanges – have

an incentive to develop appropriate regulatory systems in ways that reduce the cost of capital to companies. On the one hand, they will not want to impose unnecessary cost burdens on listed companies and participants in the market. On the other hand, they will want to ensure appropriate investor protection. Exchanges are in a perfect position to balance these two objectives appropriately.

- Traditional objections to private regulation of investment markets are generally not now valid. In particular, it can no longer be argued that exchanges are natural monopolies – there is global competition. The race-to-the-bottom argument is false: exchanges will develop rules systems that produce the lowest cost of capital, not the weakest mechanisms of investor protection. Indeed, the FSA has made statements that implicitly accept the idea that market-based regulation could be effective.

- Statutory regulators are monopolies that are riddled with 'public choice' problems. Incentives are poorly aligned within regulators.

- Previous proposals to 'abolish' the FSA, such as those on which the Conservative Party fought the last general election, which now form coalition plans, have involved nothing of the sort. In effect we have a proposal for the creation of a huge regulator which would also be responsible for the conduct of monetary policy – the 'FSA' will be a subsidiary of the 'Bank of England'. The authors believe that the other responsibilities of the FSA (consumer protection, insurance regulation, banking regulation and so on) should be abandoned or, in limited cases, dispersed. As such the FSA really can be abolished.

- It might be possible to make some progress by following proposals in the Liberal Democrat 2010 election manifesto for the creation of regional stock exchanges that are exempt from FSA and EU regulation. There could also be complete liberalisation of the Alternative Investment Market (AIM).

BOXES AND TABLE

Does Britain Need a Financial Regulator?

1 INTRODUCTION

The great Austrian economist Ludwig von Mises, mentor of F. A. Hayek, was once asked at what point on the line between freedom and statism would he designate a country as socialist or not (Rothbard, 1995: ch. 103). His answer was that a good barometer would be whether or not there was a stock market; without a stock market there can be no genuine private ownership of capital: with one there can be no true socialism.

This may be a good answer if one is put on the spot, but what if the stock market is controlled by the government? Perhaps we can deduce that Mises would have said the country was then socialist – it is certainly not fully capitalist.

On this criterion the UK is very much in the balance: one of the main features of a stock exchange on which companies 'list' and via which participants trade is the rules under which such listings and trading operate. In the London Stock Exchange, rules are controlled by the Financial Services Authority, an arm of the government; a similar situation exists for the New York Stock Exchange.

Another barometer of the situation may be corporate governance. Most corporations are free market entities only to the extent that their owners can devise the ways in which they (peacefully) behave. Corporate governance is not yet completely controlled by the government but it is certainly reaching the point where the word corporatist can reasonably be used.

This monograph examines whether a single blow could be a force for freedom by making competitive, freely functioning stock exchanges an effective arm of corporate governance via their rules on listing and trading. It is not a treatise on regulation as such (other IEA publications, such as Blundell and Robinson, 2000, explore this question). Nor is it a treatise on corporate governance as such (again, IEA publications such as Sternberg, 2004, have dealt with these issues). Instead, while it does have wider considerations and refers to them from time to time, this monograph has the more limited objective of asking whether investment market regulation could sit more firmly in the private sector alongside other private institutions carrying on similar work. For example, could competitive stock exchanges and shareholder governance find better ways of dealing with insider trading than the approaches of the FSA and the SEC (the US Securities and Exchange Commission)? As we shall show, it is not only history which answers this question in the affirmative: theory is equally compelling.

After this Introduction, we look briefly at the functions of the FSA and argue that they should be abolished or passed to other arms of government in very diminished forms. We then trace the evolution of the London Stock Exchange and the state's seizure of its supervisory freedom before examining the experience of stock markets overseas. The following two chapters look at the development of statutory regulation and then the now-dominant role of the European Union is discussed. The later chapters examine the respective economic arguments for and against regulation by the market and conclude that it is far superior to regulation by statutory authorities. The underlying reason for this is that statutory authorities (ultimately answerable to politicians) have no incentives to strike balances, to provide a diversity of solutions or to evolve alongside market discoveries. It was ever thus. We also show that the commonsense view that competition among stock exchanges, each with their different regulatory approaches, produces a race to the top and not to the bottom is indeed correct. Yes, an exchange may wish to stop short of suspending a listed company for misbehaving because of the revenue it loses, but it needs investors as well as companies, and the former can walk away too. More generally we are amazed at the manner in which stock exchanges are treated as being a world apart from other businesses, requiring special controls from on high. And again, as we shall show, while financial scandals do appear to be longer and more frequent than in other areas of business, the major reason is that state regulation begets them – it has certainly done nothing to diminish them.

2 APART FROM INVESTMENT MARKET REGULATION, WHAT ELSE SHOULD THE FSA NOT BE DOING?

This monograph is primarily about the regulation of investment markets. It makes the rather bold claim, however, that the UK Financial Services Authority (FSA) should be abolished. What should happen to the other functions of the FSA? On the face of it, other proposals have been made to abolish the FSA too. For example, the Conservative Party (Conservative Party, 2009) proposed moving the powers for the supervision of financial institutions into the Bank of England while creating a Consumer Protection Agency to regulate the selling process of financial firms. The plan has been revised by the coalition government, but is still broadly the same. The plan abolishes the FSA in theory but, in practice, will simply divide the institution in two – moving one half into the Bank of England while the other half will be a new quango concerned with consumer protection. Astonishingly, the 57-page document spelling out the Conservatives' pre-election policy dealt with investment market regulation, which is perhaps one third of the FSA's work and budget, in only one paragraph:

> We will consult on which regulatory authority should take
> on the FSA's various other responsibilities including markets
> and securities regulation, 'approved persons' licensing and
> listing authority responsibilities. For example, markets
> regulation could be combined with the Takeover Panel and
> Financial Reporting Council to streamline the number of

> regulators and create a powerful markets authority akin to
> that in France, Italy, Spain, Portugal and most of Eastern
> Europe. We will consult on this idea. (Ibid.: 49)

So, this would have led to the creation of a third FSA to complement 'FSA1', which would have had responsibility for consumer protection, and 'FSA2', which would be a subsidiary of the Bank of England. The Conservative Party did not, in fact, propose abolition of the FSA and a return of its functions to the market but a rearrangement of its functions. Indeed, a Conservative Party Treasury shadow minister has said: 'We want to see a much more intrusive regime by the Bank of England',[1] so it seems that increasing the degree of statutory regulation yet further is the aim of the Conservative government. It now seems likely that the regulation of financial markets will be undertaken alongside a consumer protection function under the revised plans.

Some regulatory reform will happen, with the Bank of England being given some additional powers. Certainly there is no liberalisation planned. In this context of regulatory change, we discuss in brief what we believe should happen to the other areas of financial regulation that are not the main focus of this monograph. This is not done to provide an in-depth analysis of each aspect but to make clear that there is a prima facie case to be made that the other aspects of FSA work can be slimmed down and transferred to private bodies or pre-existing statutory bodies. As a result, we can safely conclude that the FSA can be abolished – not merged with the Bank of England or replicated two or three times over, but abolished.

---

1 See: http://uk.reuters.com/article/idUKTRE59D2B320091014 (accessed 29 October 2009).

Regulation of banks

The authors have sympathy with models of free banking without central banks along the lines proposed by Austrian economists. We do not make that case here, however – it is the subject of a fierce debate, even among free-market economists. Instead, for the sake of argument, we take the existing central banking arrangements as given. From that starting point, it makes sense for the central bank to be the regulator of those banks connected directly to the payments system and, in return, the central bank would be the provider of lender-of-last-resort facilities. The central bank should have its capital provided by the private sector along the lines discussed in Congdon (2009) and could run a deposit insurance scheme. If these reforms are put in place, then the incentives for the central bank would tend to lead to a more appropriate degree of regulation than currently comes from the FSA. The extent of regulation would not be determined by bureaucratic fiat with all the problems that brings with it. Instead, regulation would be designed by the central bank trading off the costs of regulation to its shareholders (the clearing banks) and the benefits regulation brings in terms of reducing the risk to the deposit insurance fund and to the Bank itself as lender of last resort. There would then be a clear economic rationale for banking regulation, as there used to be before it was undertaken by the FSA. The focus of regulation could once again become the protection of the payments system, while allowing individual banks to fail in an orderly fashion.

Regulation of insurance companies

For 100 years from 1870, insurance companies in the UK had very limited regulation. The system worked. Insolvencies of life insurance companies were very, very rare events and policy-holders rarely – if ever – suffered. Companies used to compete not just on the bonuses they paid but on how *conservative* they were (see Booth, 2007). Non-life insurance insolvencies were more common but did not give rise to serious catastrophes, and the market in the UK was vibrant and competitive. It is interesting that within twenty years of the regulation of life insurance companies becoming much more prescriptive, we had the problem with Equitable Life. Particular methods of accounting for liabilities became statutorily approved and these methods became fossilised and antique.[2]

The authors believe that we should simply return to a system of insurance regulation that requires extensive disclosure to the market with the 'regulator' merely acting as the intermediary by which this disclosure takes place. This could be managed by a small division of a government ministry. An additional provision requiring complex insurance companies to issue subordinated debt that turned into equity in the event of insolvency might also be useful. The new style of regulation, being implemented across the European Union, under the so-called Solvency II agenda, repeats exactly the same mistakes that have been made by both banking regulators and banks' managers over the last few years. Complex models are going to be used to determine how much capital individual insurance companies should keep. The learning process within regulatory bureaus is slow!

---

2   Two additional points are of interest here. First, some would argue that Equitable Life's problems led to insolvency only because of a mistaken judgement of the House of Lords. Second, the regulators' handling of the crisis has been strongly criticised in government reports (see: http://news.bbc.co.uk/1/shared/bsp/hi/pdfs/17_07_08_equitable.pdf).

Regulation of investment banks and complex financial companies – the AIG problem

One of the reasons for creating the FSA was because it was believed that the integration of financial markets required a 'one-stop shop' for financial regulation. It might appear that the problems that were experienced in the insurance group AIG – which had been involved with credit derivatives and was saved to prevent the failure of banks – would give strength to that argument. The economic reasons for regulating banks, however, are different from the weaker economic case for regulating insurance companies and investment banks. If a commercial bank fails then, the argument proceeds, it can bring down other banks and cause the payments system to collapse. The case has now been made that this applies to other financial institutions – such as AIG. Thus, it is said, the collapse of AIG could have brought down an investment bank and this could, in turn, have led to a wider collapse of the financial system.

This concern seems to be at the heart of moves by the EU to try to regulate hedge funds and other private investment funds to a greater degree.[3] There is no suggestion that they were in any way responsible for the financial crash, but concerns are expressed that the failure of a hedge fund could bring down a bank that had lent to it. But drawing the regulatory net wider and wider simply encourages financial institutions to become more and more complex and is highly inefficient. It would make more sense for the regulator of commercial banks – we have suggested the Bank of England – to ensure that banks are appropriately regulated where they have risky counterparties. Thus, if a bank

---

3   Through the Alternative Investment Fund Managers Directive.

has significant exposure to an investment bank and the investment bank, in turn, is exposed to the failure of one or more hedge funds, then this may be a reason for the regulator of the commercial banking system to take appropriate action in relation to the narrow range of banks it regulates: this is simply a case of looking down the right end of the telescope.

There is no limit to the power one could give regulators according to the logic currently being employed to support the EU Directive on alternative investment funds. What would happen if Marks & Spencer borrowed sufficient money from a particular bank that its failure would impair the solvency of that bank? Should the FSA regulate the activities of Marks & Spencer on the grounds that its failure could bring down a bank? Of course it should not. This is clearly an issue for the regulator of the bank that has lent the money in the first place. The same applies to hedge funds and complex financial institutions. If a bank has made risky loans to a hedge fund so that its failure could imperil the solvency of the bank, then that is not a reason to bring hedge funds into the regulatory net. The matter should be considered by the regulator of the banking system. Thus, in short, we are extremely sceptical of proposals to have extensive financial regulation and regulatory capital requirements on investment banks, hedge funds and complex financial institutions. If a financial institution carries on both banking and other business, then there is a case for requiring different types of business to take place in different subsidiaries, but this already happens to a large degree.

Regulation of the sale of financial products

This monograph is not about the regulation of the sale of retail financial products. This is an important function of the FSA, however, and forms a main plank of the coalition proposals discussed above. The authors believe that special financial regulators are not needed here. Until recently, contract law, common law and the occasional specific Act of Parliament regulated the sale of financial products. Specific financial regulation raises costs and particularly damages the sale of products to low-income households. Improvements could be made to the legal system in this regard. Greater use of class actions, a more activist role for the courts in interpreting misleading terms and conditions of sale and, possibly, a body to take up court actions on behalf of consumers might well lead to much better practice in financial markets. There seems to be no evidence that the statutory regulation of the sale of financial products has achieved much at all – except imposing great costs on consumers – and this is not a function that needs to be carried out by a regulatory bureau.[4] The FSA had no regulatory authority over the sale of mortgages or general insurance until 2005.[5] Before then, the UK had very competitive mortgage and general insurance markets with no obvious problems that needed to be addressed by statutory

4   Readers might point out the mis-selling 'scandals'. Two of the major mis-selling scandals (zero-dividend preference shares and endowment mortgages) happened only because of the perverse tax treatment of certain financial products. The other major mis-selling scandal (personal pensions) happened because the government passed legislation retrospectively allowing employees to break contracts of employment and leave company pension schemes. In any case, if a customer is misled in the selling process, courts could simply declare contracts to be unenforceable. It is doubtful that such a change would even require primary legislation.

5   As has been noted by others, the purchase of a £20,000 car simply involves common law, contract law and some specific primary legislation. The sale of a £300 insurance policy with the car involves a huge amount of point-of-sale regulation generated by the FSA.

regulation. The occasional problem in relation to competition and inappropriate selling procedures and so on could be, and was,[6] dealt with by the Office of Fair Trading and/or the Competition Commission.

Regulation of pension funds

Until 1995, the basic principle of a defined-benefit pension fund was that the trustees used the funds in the best financial interests of members. If there was insufficient money to pay all the pensions that had been 'promised' then 'promises' could be scaled back. It was felt, however, that this did not give sufficient security to members. This is a pity because even if a fund suffered a shortfall, under the pre-1995 arrangements, all members would – except in extreme circumstances – have only a small reduction in their pension entitlements. The 1995 Pensions Act then required trustees to impose all the shortfall of the fund on people who were not yet in receipt of a pension. This meant that a specific sub-group of people were now at risk of losing a much larger sum of money if a fund had a deficit. In response to some specific scandals, the government then acted to require a much higher funding level of pension funds and also required employers to purchase a form of insurance. Greater regulation of pension funds through a statutory regulator (though not the FSA) soon followed. These requirements followed two decades during which more statutory obligations to increase benefits were imposed upon pension funds.

The history of trust-based pension funds from 1921 to 1995

---

6   And, indeed, still is.

shows that additional regulation is simply not needed. Trust law will suffice. It was the Maxwell scandal which brought about the changes in the law in 1995. The Maxwell scandal involved an already illegal reallocation of pension fund money, however. The experience since 1995 suggests that increased statutory regulation – together with other trends in the world of finance and in financial markets – has led to the 'pursuit of the perfect being the enemy of the good'. Since 1995, defined-benefit pension funds have declined dramatically in the private sector. This tried-and-tested method of providing pensions was not good enough for the government and regulators – private pensions had to be 'perfected'. The pursuit of this perfection led to their elimination. There is little left to regulate, sadly, except a declining book of old schemes.

Though it may not lead to a revival of the pre-1995 success of defined-benefit pension schemes, we would argue that no statutory regulation of pensions is necessary except through basic primary law and trust law. There should be no role for the FSA in the regulation of defined-benefit pension funds; nor are other regulatory bodies needed either.

Conservative proposals relating to the regulation of investment activity

Having dismissed, albeit briefly, the case for FSA regulation of financial services and financial markets in most areas, we are left with the main focus of this monograph – the regulation of investment markets. The Conservative Party proposed merging the FSA regulation of investment markets with the Financial Reporting Council or the Takeover Panel to create a single powerful regulatory body for investment markets. The extent to which these last two bodies should have statutory power is a moot point. These Conservative Party proposals seem, however, to lead to precisely the same problems that arose from the creation of the FSA. The coalition's new proposals are no better in this respect. A single, powerful, statutory regulatory monopoly would have no focus nor natural incentives to regulate appropriately – the bureaucratic mentality would dominate. Second, the proposals fail to recognise the extraordinarily rich history of stock exchanges as private institutions that generate their own regulatory framework. It is to this issue that we turn in the rest of the monograph.

Conclusion

We would argue that, in so far as regulation is necessary in other areas for which the FSA has responsibility, this regulation would be better done by different bodies in a way compatible with the rule of law and governed by appropriate economic incentives. Theory and evidence suggest, however, that most areas of financial regulation do not need special statutory bodies with wide-ranging powers. Our proposals with regard to the regulation of investment markets would pull the heart out of the FSA, which should then be disbanded, with remaining functions being either made redundant or being passed to other bodies which would have better incentives to regulate appropriately.

3 THE EVOLUTION OF STOCK EXCHANGE REGULATION IN THE UK

Stock exchanges as privately regulated institutions

> Once upon a time, three hundred years ago, the City of
> London was a stronghold of radicalism, an outpost of the
> Left.

Hugh Dalton, October 1945

In his widely acclaimed history of the London Stock Exchange (Michie, 1999), Ranald Michie defines a stock exchange as a market where specialist intermediaries buy and sell securities under a common set of rules and regulations through a closed system dedicated to that purpose. The exchange guarantees that a transaction can be fulfilled even if there are no matched buyers and sellers. He goes on to argue that the London Stock Exchange has come under increasing state control, broadly throughout the twentieth century, and certainly since the 1980s. It has had to rediscover its role without the second leg of his definition. In other words, its general regulatory functions, which allowed it to differentiate itself from other forums, have been hijacked by state regulators.

This situation is similar in most of the Western world, and the nature of both stock exchanges and 'other trading forums' is constantly changing owing not only to regulation but also to technological development. Indeed, we doubt that any expert could meaningfully lay down *sine qua non*s or differentiators that would separate the definitions of each type of exchange or forum, certainly not in a way that would withstand the test of even a few years. What is important for our discussion is whether or not trading entities or stock exchanges with rules as to both listing and trading of securities will themselves remain. We believe that we can be confident that the answer is 'yes' (Morgan Stanley and Mercer Oliver Wyman, 2003), although the precise form that they will take cannot be predicted and should not be enshrined in state regulation.

The more commonly asked question is 'are stock exchanges monopolies?' There is concern that stock exchanges can operate restrictive practices as effective monopolies. The formal answer to this question is 'no' (see below). New ways can always be developed for individuals and institutions to exchange or trade securities that bypass formal exchanges or which use different forms of exchange, and this is becoming increasingly common. As such, technological development leaves state regulation looking more and more moribund. For example, in the UK, the Alternative Investment Market demonstrates that there will always be a market for lighter regulation, especially if heavier regulation is inappropriate and misdirected. As various other new trading platforms also demonstrate, there is a large market for trading without listing on exchanges at all, partly propelled by expensive and largely irrelevant state regulation of stock exchanges. Unless simple changes of stock ownership are to be entirely banned outside an approved route (which many fear will be the outcome of the application of EU regulations) then there is no question that traditional stock exchanges must always heed competition.

Stock exchanges and private regulation in the UK

For our purposes, then, relevant history relates to stock exchanges as currently understood, namely exchanges with market-makers, transaction guarantees, publishing full transaction records, and carrying listing and trading rules. In the UK this is encapsulated by the London Stock Exchange (LSE), which began life as such an exchange in 1801. By 1825 it was on the way to becoming a world institution, helping to create an integrated global economy via global capital movement. This journey carried on through the halcyon days of laissez-faire capitalism, or liberalism as the term was then understood, until World War I.

Overseas stock exchanges will be discussed below. It is important to note here, however, that the history of the development of the privately regulated London exchange is not just an accident of time, place and circumstances. We will draw similar lessons from the development of exchanges in central and eastern Europe. But, arguably, the London exchange was the world's first stock exchange according to Michie's definition (i.e. including formal rules and appropriate disciplines on the conduct of business). It successfully blended 'the need for access and participation with that of control over the conduct of members' (Michie, 1999: 3). Over the next 100 years the LSE was unquestionably a great success story and became the world's premier stock market with a huge international reputation and international business to match. At the same time, several regional stock markets also thrived.

The precursors of the London Stock Exchange (LSE) were the informal exchanges in coffee shops in the eighteenth century. These also developed systems of rules and enforcement. Those who did not settle their accounts were 'named and shamed' and labelled 'lame duck'. Punishment involved banishment from acting as brokers in the coffee houses. A crucial aspect of the development of more formal exchanges was the ability to discriminate. This ability to discriminate is still important today – an exchange must be allowed to set up its own rules for entry and have its own punishments for disobeying the rules. There is a long and successful tradition of such private rule-making, based on the principle of freedom of contract, in the UK, not just in financial exchanges but also in sports clubs and associations. Interestingly, throughout the exchange's early history, pressure was put on government to prevent the exchange from restricting entry only to those who were willing to abide by the rules. Indeed, it is also interesting that the demise of the London Stock Exchange as an independent self-regulatory body began with an inquiry into exactly that issue 180 years later.

Members were fined if they broke the rules and Stringham (2002) comments that fines for breaking the rules were put to charitable purposes. This would seem to be an effective mechanism to align the interests of members and the rule-making committee – rather better than using the money for the benefit of the exchange.

After the exchange moved to Capel Court in 1801 the brokers who were excluded from the exchange again petitioned the government to force the exchange to open up to all members of the public – indeed, a parliamentary Bill was drafted to that effect (ibid.). The opponents of the Bill argued that its purpose was to provide shelter to fraudsters – if private rules could not be enforced, then the exchange would not be able to maintain the reputation such institutions need to thrive.

There might have been a genuine fear that the exchange could act as a cartel. If it did so, however, and if its rules were simply designed to restrict competition, the exchange would not have survived: there was no impediment to prevent rival exchanges from establishing themselves. Reading contemporary accounts, it seems clear that the regulation that the LSE brought in was appropriate to and kept up with the environment of the time. It was not designed to restrict competition. Both companies whose shares were quoted on the market and exchange members (jobbers and brokers) were regulated in order to ensure that their dealings were transparent – thus enhancing the reputation of the exchange (see, for example, Burns, 1909). Unlike under today's FSA monopoly regime, transactions in securities could also take place in unregulated environments among non-members. There is little evidence that this created serious problems, and any investor would be able to distinguish clearly between members and non-members of the exchange: membership was an important marketing device – there was a 'race to the top' in regulation.

Competition – actual and potential – between rules systems was possible. For example, new rules were introduced in 1909 that made clear the requirement for the separation of dealing and broking in order that a transactor would have no doubt on whose behalf a broker was acting.[1] This was to remain a pillar of the London exchange until 'Big Bang' in 1986. Other rules were simultaneously introduced to prevent conflicts of interest. There was some opposition to the rule changes and rumours about the possibility of a new exchange with less inhibiting rules did circulate. Competition between rules systems was more than a theoretical possibility, despite the technological limitations of the time.

---

1   See *The Times*, 1 February 1909, reproduced in Burns (1909).

In similar vein, Paul Mahoney (Mahoney, 1997), mainly describing the development of the New York Stock Exchange but referring also to others, is able to say:

> In summary, many stock exchange rules in the era before governmental regulation were premised on the idea that to attract investors, the exchange had to provide elementary protection against defaults, forgeries, fraud, manipulation and other avoidable risks. Thus stock exchange rules dealt with most of the broad categories of issues with which modern securities regulations are concerned.

The decline of private regulation

In both the USA and the UK, the political clamour for government regulation arose from a financial crisis – primarily the 1929 stock market crash in the USA and the abandoning of the gold standard in the UK in 1931. Mahoney examines the arguments for the formation of the Securities and Exchange Commission (SEC) and finds them wanting. At that time no body similar to the SEC was formed in the UK – it wasn't 'necessary' because World War I 'had witnessed an unprecedented increase in State control of the affairs of the Stock Exchange, and these controls were maintained in place when peace came'. Although there were some gradual relaxations, 'Behind the scenes the Treasury and the Bank of England, either singly or jointly, continued to exert an influence in the manner they had become accustomed to during the war' (Michie, 1999: 182).

The new creed of big government had arrived, a creed which intensified (certainly in the UK) in the interwar period. The old trust and stability of the liberal era had gone and between the wars the LSE was controlled increasingly by its members (who had previously shared it with the proprietors), resulting in a members' buyout in 1947.

In the LSE, 'members' were stockjobbers and stockbrokers. The former were owners of stock, specifically for the purposing of holding it for periods until a buyer could be found to match a seller or vice versa. Brokers did not own stock and were essentially intermediaries who usually specialised in particular companies, types of company or types of security.

Membership was individual and their firms were partnerships. There can be no doubt that one of the major factors in the decline of this system, in particular the stockjobbers, was the punitive taxation (especially income tax) that grew remorselessly after both world wars. As pointed out by both Michie (1999) and Kynaston (2002), this made individual capital accumulation almost impossible, and it is ironic that the large investment corporations that are vilified by many supporters of big government were brought into being by that same big government.

For 30 years after World War II, the LSE then receded almost entirely from its former international role (mostly as a result of exchange controls and other post-war regulations). Perhaps the most striking feature of this period, however, was the enormous influence of the Bank of England, nationalised in 1946 and the first all-powerful 'City' regulator. Its will (and via it, the government's) may have been imparted with highly refined nods and winks by highly refined and polite individuals, but there is no mistaking the steel behind them. It seems likely that this was not Kynaston's intention, but his book (ibid.) makes the fact startlingly clear. This influence was often nationalistic, conservative and 'old school tie', and did much to preserve City monopolies and cartels. The Bank was also incompetent on a significant number of occasions.

Another striking feature of the post-war period is the raising of the spectre of a US-style Securities and Exchange Commission, usually as a stick with which to beat opposition to proposed additional controls. This commission, formed under President Roosevelt in 1934, was, and remains, a fearsome state regulator in a land of supposed free enterprise. From the very beginning it adopted the 'self-regulatory organisation' (SRO) model, which turned from spectre to reality in the UK 50 years later and which is usually described as 'part of the private-enterprise system' when clearly it is nothing of the sort (this topic is discussed further below). So, from the end of World War I onwards, we have an elegant private regulatory institution gradually becoming part of a set of cartels and corporatist institutions.

The build-up to Big Bang – death by a thousand cuts

By 1979 the LSE was under irresistible pressure to change. As mentioned above, there was a major shortage of jobbers and capital and 'put through' deals (bypassing jobbers) were commonplace. There was unrest about commission levels (after Wall Street had abandoned its fixed commissions) and the (by now dominant) institutional investors were particularly irritated about the high commission payable to the few select brokers who were selling gilts on the back of an explosion in government debt.

The Office of Fair Trading was beginning to flex its muscles and Roy Hattersley had extended the Fair Trading Act to the service sector; in 1979 he formally referred the LSE to the Restrictive Practices Court. The Gower Report, at the time the latest of several statutory investigations of the stock exchange, was clearly going to castigate its 'self-regulatory system' (which it duly did in 1984) and the stock exchange's restrictive practices were driving companies away.

In 1982 the Restrictive Practices Court assailed the separation of capacity (jobbing and broking discussed above) and the National Association of Pension Funds was attacking the commission system with gusto: the attacks on the rules systems did not just come from arms of government. The LSE remained in limbo until 1983 when its chairman, Nicholas Goodison, and the Secretary of State for Trade, Cecil Parkinson, reached a deal to call off the Restrictive Practices Court and to dismantle minimum commissions by 1986. Thereafter deals involving the purchase of brokers and jobbers came thick and fast, with the Bank of England smiling on anything that might stave off the threat of US domination (Kynaston, 2002: 637). Enormous mistakes were made both in the run-up to Big Bang (October 1986) and thereafter. By 1995 it had become clear that 'the better strategy had been the non-integrated, niche approach' (ibid.) – a major reason being that many of those who had pursued mergers and acquisitions became diverted, losing money as well as focus.

David Kynaston cites Tim Congdon, writing in *The Spectator* a week before Big Bang that: 'The Big Bang is said to be necessary to improve the City's international competitiveness ... It would be more accurate to say that the LSE has lost ground relative to the Eurobond market and that a change in rules is necessary ... This is the sense in which the Big Bang is a by-product of the Bigger Bang.' It would have been much better, we would argue, to allow the London Stock Exchange to take its own decisions without governmental pressure.

After the publication of the Gower Report in 1984 and the Financial Services Act 1986, the so-called 'self-regulatory' system was put in place, in the shape of the Securities and Investments Board (SIB), responsible for supervising the financial markets with the help of the now infamous alphabet soup of 'self-regulators' (separate regulators for fund managers (IMRO), life insurance companies (LAUTRO) and so on). Scandals continued unabated into the 1990s, until eventually in 1997 Chancellor Gordon Brown removed the satellite deckchairs and created the Financial Services Authority, which would take on 2,000 staff in the following three years, ready for the Financial Services and Markets Act (FSMA) 2000. We examine the current regulatory environment, including the growing role of the European Union, in later chapters.

AIM: a competing market

AIM (Alternative Investment Market) began life in 1995 to replace the Unlisted Securities Market. AIM is owned and regulated by the London Stock Exchange and its Listing Rules are *not* directly controlled by the government or the FSA; it is 'Exchange-regulated'. It is also one of the most successful markets in the world, and hosts more companies than its parent. It is host or co-host to a large number of non-UK companies (approximately 12 per cent of its total), and is being copied in several other countries.

Why? A lighter regulatory touch is the primary reason. (As mentioned below, this does *not* mean that companies can get away with far too much – if that were the case it would have lots of companies but no investors!) As Henry Angest, the chairman of Arbuthnot Banking Group, pointed out in a letter to the *Financial*

Times on 14 July 2005, explaining the company's move to AIM, it means that companies are relieved of the LSE's 'inflated reporting requirements', which force companies to provide at huge cost book-sized annual reports which nobody reads other than the self-appointed proxy agencies.

The main mechanism is AIM's NOMAD (Nominated Adviser) system in which each company has a broker or accounting firm as an adviser with the responsibility for meeting listing requirements.

The requirements that have to be met before shares can be traded on AIM are relatively simple. Advisers and brokers have to be appointed and admissions documents prepared (to include information on all activities of the company, financial information and projections). For example, unlike in the main market, there is no minimum number of shares that has to be held in public hands (25 per cent on the main market); no trading record (three years for the main market); and no minimum market capitalisation (£0.7 million on the main market). To continue trading, a number of conditions have to be met, laid down by AIM and not by government regulations. For example, half-yearly and annual accounts have to be published. These accounts must follow UK or US generally accepted accounting practice or international accounting standards. Directors and applicable employees cannot deal during a market 'close' period. Directors are responsible for compliance with the rules. If rules are not followed, shares can be suspended from AIM.

Other exchanges and electronic markets

AIM involves product diversification from a given exchange

provider. There are competing exchanges too, of course. Companies do not need to have their shares traded on their domestic exchange and transnational companies can have multiple listings on different exchanges with different listing rules and regulatory frameworks. Electronic markets, such as Chi-X and Turquoise, also provide competition as trading platforms. Unfortunately, however, because the service of providing the package of rules and regulations to govern trading has been taken over by the government, the one thing these markets cannot do is compete according to their regulatory frameworks. In general, the rules for membership are heavily driven by government regulatory rules and the exchanges very much focus on competing on the basis of their charging structure. Competing on the basis of charges is, of course, perfectly valid and welcome, but the authors believe that an important function of the market is lost when competition on the basis of regulatory frameworks is downplayed.

Conclusion

The development of self-regulating and self-policing exchanges in the UK was remarkable. Methods of enforcement, risk management and the detailed regulations evolved to cope with changing circumstances, changing technology and the needs of different types of company and investors. There is no question that the regulation of investment transactions is needed if securities markets are to achieve any great volume of trades. The question is 'Who should regulate?' Stringham (2002) concludes: 'While it may be the case [that] the regulation of a stock market is necessary there is no reason to conclude that it must be done by the state.' The historical evidence surveyed above supports that view. The theory discussed below does so too.

4 STOCK EXCHANGES AROUND THE WORLD

The experience of stock exchanges in the UK is not unique – though it probably provides the best example of the private regulation of investment markets. It is also worth examining briefly other investment markets – both historically and, in the case of post-communist countries, in more recent times.

The USA

The USA lost much of its freedom in 1934 with the birth of the Securities and Exchange Commission (SEC) and its fearsome powers, often cited in the UK over the next 50 years or so as a means of achieving obeisance to the government and the Bank of England. In practice the relative historical success of US stock exchanges, the New York Stock Exchange (NYSE) in particular, was due to the flexibility in SEC interpretations and administration (Mahoney, 1997) – a flexibility that is now being used in draconian ways.

It is now clear that prior to the SEC, the NYSE and other US exchanges made a pretty good fist of regulating their listed companies and their members, and that the formation of the SEC was a politically motivated reaction to the Great Depression, the seeds of which were created by government, not financial markets, during a credit-creation spree in the 1920s (Rothbard, 1983).

The underlying arguments for and against state regulation in the USA are well captured by Mahoney (1997). As in the UK, the monopoly argument can be short-circuited by the clear presence of competition for trading (Beny, 2001), with half a dozen or so traditional-style exchanges plus NASDAQ and electronic platforms such as Instinet. Switching is by no means uncommon.

The incentives for regulation by exchanges (versus regulations by politicians and bureaucrats) are, as ever, that exchanges want to do business and extend liquidity whereas bureaucrats require political results which are a function of transient features. In *normal* circumstances the latter has led to collusion with business in regulatory capture (the SEC regulated the NYSE for 40 years without seeking to remove its fixed commissions) while *abnormal* circumstances (nearly always market crashes, when investors are already hugely risk-averse) lead to hyperactivity and ill-judged reforms such as the Sarbanes-Oxley Act or SOX (Romano, 2005).

Mahoney gives short shrift to the argument that a stock exchange would have little resolve to seriously punish a listed wrongdoer (who may then defect to a competing exchange) with a simple rejoinder: exchanges need *investors* as well as companies, and investors are hardly likely to favour such capitulation. Furthermore, there is evidence that competition for order-flow among market centres is *beneficial* to overall liquidity (Boehmer and Boehmer, 2002).

Thus, as in the UK, there seems to be no obvious case for government regulation of investment markets in the USA. It was brought in as a misguided reaction to the Great Depression and seems to have all the faults one would expect of government regulation.

In the USA, competition between regulators in different states is theoretically possible. The role of the states as possible competitive regulators is examined in Roberta Romano's paper 'Is regulatory competition a problem or irrelevant for corporate governance?' (Romano, 2005). She notes that the states are competing for investment business. As a result, where they have the authority, they carry out regular reviews leading to experimentation and policy innovation (something sadly lacking at federal level) and they usually offer a 'menu' of regulations, whereas the SEC (and other federal regulators and governments around the world) has mandatory requirements. In the opinion of Romano (and many other researchers), SOX was a 'legislative blunder', politically motivated and almost wholly irrelevant to its alleged causes, the Enron and WorldCom scandals.

Hong Kong

According to Hong Kong's Independent Commission Against Corruption (ICAC), few cities better fit the description of a financial centre. It goes on to say that its enviable reputation for its rule of law and well-regulated financial sector was not necessarily the case in the city's stock market up until the late 1980s, and describes a major listing scam that occurred within a few months of the Stock Exchange of Hong Kong's (SEHK) establishment in 1986.

It may or may not be a coincidence that prior to that listing scam there were *four* competing Hong Kong stock exchanges. Although there had been only one Hong Kong Stock Exchange from 1947, the late 1960s saw that market begin to play an increasingly important role in corporate capital-raising, and three more exchanges opened between 1969 and 1973 – all with different listing requirements, rules and practices. But, shortly after 1974, according to researchers at King's College Management Centre (Ho et al., 2004), 'the need to rationalise the four Stock Exchanges naturally became apparent', even though none of the three newcomers had lived for more than a few years! The 'flaws in the market' revealed in 1987 appear to offer no lesson to the researchers except that more state regulation was necessary (it was forthcoming in 1998), despite the ending of competition almost before it had begun, and despite the facts that the unified exchange was formed and opened 'after much deliberation' and that its opening was immediately followed by a major listing scandal.

What a pity that a major opportunity to study competitive exchanges and competition in rule-making was cut off just after birth. The regulation of the SEHK (the tenth-largest in the world) appears to follow the all-too-familiar path, boasting a Securities and Futures Commission (SFC) with full legal powers, including prosecution, the usual anti-insider dealing regime, and plans to be the sole listing regulator (indeed, the sole financial services regulator) modelled on our own Financial Services Authority. These proposals are presented by the SFC as being 'in line with the wishes of the market', despite a prior submission by the exchange taking a contrary view.

Singapore

Singapore holds out more hope in that the Singapore Stock Exchange (SGX) is not only a listed company but is also responsible for its own rules and enforcement thereof, although it is ultimately answerable to the courts under the Securities and Futures

Act, which at least maintains the separation of powers that is crumbling elsewhere, not least in the UK.

Since 1999 the SGX has been split into a profit-seeking commercial arm and a non-profit regulatory arm, rather like the SROs in the UK's pre-FSA regime. Again the assumption behind this is that conflicts between profits and regulation could arise, which to our minds is an unsupported claim unless the SGX is a monopoly. Our request to the SGX to clarify these points was met with a sharp and polite refusal.

Amsterdam

The Amsterdam stock market began in 1602 and soon included facilities for the future settlement of transactions, thus opening up the possibility of default. Management of settlement became a key aspect of exchanges' functions and helped maintain liquidity. It was recognised that shares that were repeatedly traded did not have to be officially transferred at the time of each trade. Thus the concept of 'settlement days', on which all bargains were settled, was introduced. Exchanges have managed the risks that are involved with clearing and settling transactions in ever more sophisticated ways, right up until the present day.

The exchange was highly innovative in terms of the products that were developed and traded (see Stringham, 2003, for an excellent review of the Amsterdam market). These products brought with them various forms of counterparty risk. It might be thought that this counterparty risk was *increased* because many of the contracts were not recognised in Dutch law or were even explicitly forbidden. The opposite is the case, however. The exchange participants themselves developed their own ways of ensuring that reputation was maintained and counterparties met their obligations. All this took place in an environment of competition against unlicensed brokers. When the government intervened with a simple ban on certain types of transaction, the brokers carried on regardless (i.e. broke the law) and continued to develop contracts that could never be enforced in law. Such contracts thrived because the market also developed rules and regulations and boycotted those without a good reputation (see Stringham and Boettke, 2004, and the references therein). The early development of the Amsterdam market is a remarkable example of spontaneous development of rules and enforcement systems in the most difficult of circumstances.

Central and eastern Europe

The post-communist countries of central and eastern Europe also provide examples that strengthen our beliefs in the advantages of self-organising and self-regulating exchanges over centralised legal and regulatory authorities. Unfortunately, of course, few post-communist countries have ever pursued the kind of economic liberalism that Britain enjoyed in the nineteenth century and thus sophisticated, self-regulating exchanges have not developed. Instead, the evidence is of a negative kind – if sophisticated, self-regulating exchanges are not allowed to develop, it is not possible for statutory regulation to replace them effectively.

Stringham and Boettke (2006), for example, examine the problem of fraud in the Czech market. They find that the courts and regulatory systems cannot deal with these problems if the market does not. The law is a highly imperfect instrument, they argue, and government regulators writing more rules does not resolve this problem. Furthermore, the political process by which regulatory bureaus are created is also highly imperfect – and these imperfections cannot be assumed away. For example, the regulatory authorities created by the Czech government did not have the requisite expertise despite attempts at reform. Furthermore, one of the acts of the Czech regulatory authority was to raise the fixed costs of regulation, thus reducing competition in investment markets to the advantage of large incumbent players.

There are other interesting lessons for countries that are developing their own stock markets which relate – in some cases tangentially – to the issues that we are discussing. Specifically:

- A stock market that is based around trading shares arising from privatisations is less likely to evolve mechanisms for dealing with corporate governance than one that emerges at first to deal with new issues because agents (shareholders) are not selecting their principals (managers). The absence of large shareholdings is likely to exacerbate this problem.
- A stock exchange needs to evolve to deal with problems that arise and cannot simply be designed by regulators for the purpose of trading privatisation shares. A sophisticated stock exchange may therefore not necessarily emerge quickly within a reforming country.
- There are serious dangers, in terms of discouraging on-exchange trading, from having too much regulation of the issue and trading of shares.
- There is, in fact, no reason why each nation-state should have its own stock exchange. Indeed, it could be argued that the erroneous belief that nation-states should have their own stock exchanges arises from the desire by

national governments to regulate what should be private exchanges.

In a separate contribution, Stringham and Boettke (2004) make two very interesting points which are certainly relevant to developed countries and emerging markets alike. First, many of the problems on emerging market exchanges have arisen against a background of government policy which is generally unsatisfactory. Examples might include activist industrial policy, the way in which privatisations have been conducted or erratic tax and monetary policy. Such policies can be very disrupting to stock exchanges and lead to excessive volatility. It is important for the government to ensure the general policy background is right if investment markets are to flourish in a privately regulated environment. Second, there should be few government constraints on information sharing and on the punishment of those who do not abide by the rules, to ensure the reputation of the exchange is not damaged. For example, it is important that the government does not, on anti-discrimination or competition grounds, prevent an exchange from excluding potential members or miscreants.

Conclusion

Around the world, governments have tended to 'nationalise' the regulatory functions of investment exchanges. Rarely has there been any strong case made for this action. Early exchanges proved able to develop their own regulatory systems, and the most significant nationalisation (in the USA) arose as a result of an erroneous understanding of the causes of the Great Depression. Where exchanges still provide regulatory functions, they do so extremely successfully. Chapters 3 and 4 have merely provided background. They have shown that private regulation is practical: later chapters will deduce that it is better. We now look at the institutional framework of statutory regulation in the UK.

5 THE LONG TENTACLES OF THE FSA

The creation of the FSA

The Financial Services Act 1986 provided the framework for regulation in the UK's securities markets until the passing of the Financial Services and Markets Act (FSMA) 2000. Most of the statutory powers for financial regulation are held by the Financial Services Authority (FSA). The FSA's predecessor under the Financial Services Act 1986 was known as the Securities and Investments Board, or SIB. It is a criminal offence to conduct 'investment business' (as defined by the Act) without authorisation or exemption by the FSA. The FSA is accountable to Parliament via the Treasury. Under the 1986 Act, so-called Self Regulating Organisations (SROs) regulated the investment business carried out by their members and were accountable to the SIB. The SROs' responsibilities have also been taken over and expanded by the FSA.

The FSA is a private company limited by guarantee. It does not, however, share most of the characteristics of private companies. In effect, it is given a statutory monopoly over all aspects of financial regulation and powers to enforce its regulation. It is accountable to the Treasury and its senior officials are appointed by the Treasury. It is, in everything but precise legal structure, a single state regulator with responsibilities for supervising and regulating all aspects of financial services provision. The

FSA levies charges on the firms it regulates to meet the costs of regulation.

While the FSA has primary authority for regulating virtually all financial services provision in the UK (for example, long-term insurance, banking and so on), we concentrate here on the FSA's role as regulator of investment market business.

The objectives of the FSA

FSMA 2000 gives the FSA general powers for rule-making, preparing and issuing codes, giving general written guidance and determining its policy and principles by reference to which it performs its other functions. Given that the FSA is allowed to behave in a way which the authority itself believes most appropriate for the purpose of meeting its objectives, it is quite clear that its position as a statutory monopoly regulator is unchallenged and unchallengeable. In effect, it therefore has the power to prevent any intermediary body such as a stock exchange from developing its own rule books and can certainly ensure that the rules developed by such a body are subservient to its own rules.

The four stated main objectives of the FSA are:

- maintaining public confidence in the financial system;
- promoting public understanding of the financial system;
- securing appropriate degrees of protection for consumers; and
- reducing the extent to which businesses within and without the perimeter may be used for a purpose connected with financial crime.

There are seven constraints on the pursuit of these objectives. These constraints include the requirement to use resources efficiently; ensuring that the burden of regulation is proportionate to the benefit; maintaining international competitiveness; facilitating innovation; and facilitating competition.

Objectives ill-defined

The objectives given to the FSA are so widely defined as to justify almost any intervention that the FSA would wish to make. The first objective, as listed above, involves maintaining public confidence, an objective that is frequently used to justify the regulation of investment transactions. But, given the economic rationale for the regulation of exchange activities discussed below, it is not clear that promoting public confidence is important. Arguably, the objective of the regulator of exchange activity (whether the regulator is a private or a government regulator) should be to promote user confidence rather than wider public confidence.

The fourth stated objective does seem to be something that is reasonable for a state authority to be involved with – the avoidance of financial crime. But it is still not clear why a government monopoly regulatory body is necessary to perform this function. At least three other options are available. It could be accepted that a private exchange would not wish to be a vehicle for financial crime – any more than a reputable shop wishes to be a vehicle for handling stolen goods: private regulation would develop to deal with this issue supported, of course, by the criminal law. Second, this issue could be handled by the imposition of specific regulation. However undesirable such regulation is, it is a long step from the establishment of a single, monopoly statutory regulator of all financial activity. Third, such criminal activity could simply be the subject of enforcement by the normal statutory authorities that deal with all other criminal matters. It is legitimate, however, to call into question the meaning of the words 'financial crime' in this context. Whereas, for example, laundering money that has been gained through illegal means, fraud, etc., may be regarded by most people as activities that should be subject to the criminal law, other aspects of 'financial crime' such as insider dealing or 'manipulating a market' have their effects generally internalised within the exchange users and need not be criminal activities at all but activities that could be regulated by exchanges themselves.

The seven constraints on the FSA's activities would not appear to be effective. Indeed, the provisions relating to competition and the relationship between the FSA and the Office of Fair Trading are complex (see Alcock, 2000: ch. 3), but it is quite clear that, while the FSA is required to facilitate both innovation and competition, this does not apply to innovation and competition in regulatory mechanisms themselves!

Enforcement mechanisms

The FSA has well-defined powers of enforcement through a tribunal system. An alternative private system of regulation would require mechanisms of enforcement of its rules too – as, for example, the Football Association has in relation to its members and footballers employed by its members. From time to time, such private regulatory bodies are investigated by the European Commission or the competition authorities (though, as we have noted, this causes problems) or taken to court by those affected by their judgements, and thus private systems of regulation have to fulfil standards required by general law. With regard to the FSA, there seems little incentive for it to adopt reasonable standards of justice given its role as a statutory monopoly regulator. This was an issue of concern when the FSMA 2000 was passing through Parliament. The precise mechanisms for enforcing rules in a competitive market for regulatory systems would be a matter for the members of those systems to determine. We will return to this issue below.

Recognition of exchanges

Recognised Investment Exchanges (RIEs) – of which the London Stock Exchange is one – are under the jurisdiction of the FSA. There is a complementary category for clearing houses which can apply to become Registered Clearing Houses (RCHs). To become an RIE, an exchange must satisfy the FSA that it meets various prerequisites set out in FSMA 2000 – including having effective arrangements for monitoring and enforcing compliance with its rules. RIEs are then exempt from the need to be authorised by the FSA to carry on regulated activities in the UK. To be recognised, RIEs must comply with the Recognition Requirements of the FSMA 2000. These involve a number of requirements relating to liquidity, custody, management, record-keeping and so on. At the time of writing there were nineteen requirements in all, all of which have 'sub-requirements' generally running to between five and twenty.[1] A detailed regulatory framework is laid down

---

1   See: http://fsahandbook.info/FSA/html/handbook/REC/2/7.

relating to RIEs even though they are, technically, self-regulating. Of course, EU regulation has to be followed too.

Exchanges do not have to have RIE status but, if they do not, their employees have to subject themselves to the FSA's direct supervision and the FSA's conduct-of-business rules. In order to obtain recognition, however, the RIEs themselves have to develop rules to meet recognition requirements that are not unlike the FSA's own conduct-of-business rules.

Listing

For well over a century the oversight of listing and trading was carried out by market exchanges: private organisations. They had an incentive to produce listing requirements that were 'optimal': if they were too harsh (on listed companies) a viable market would not be created; if they were too lax, investors would not have confidence in and would not use the exchange. There was no race to the bottom in private regulation because market partici-pants demanded effective private regulation. Indeed, as is stated in FSA (2004: 5), '[W]e have applied higher standards to issuers admitted to the Official List, and our consultation has shown that market participants value many of these tougher, or super equiva-lent, standards as providing additional investor protection and contributing to deep and liquid markets.'

The function of supervising listing – the process of being admitted to the official list of shares – has now been passed to statutory bodies. The official list is today held by the UK Listing Authority (UKLA), a division of the FSA and, under the FSMA 2000, the FSA has responsibility for the regulation of companies that issue securities on the main market. It holds the 'Official

List' and controls entry to it. In 2008, the FSA approved 1,900 company prospectuses for listing.[2]

The decision for private exchanges in the UK to give up the responsibility for the official list was taken by the London Stock Exchange itself. When it decided to demutualise in 1999, it felt that it should no longer be the listing authority and it was decided to transfer this responsibility to the FSA. It was not unreasonable to be concerned about a profit-making body holding the 'Official List' and being in the monopoly position of 'gatekeeper' to the markets. It is not clear, however, why an official list is needed at all. Individual exchanges have their own requirements for companies admitted to trading which are additional to those required for admittance to the Official List. Alternatively, exchanges can choose to admit for trading companies that are not on the Official List. It appears that the FSA believes that the holding of an official list makes other aspects of its supervisory job easier because all listed companies have some contact with the FSA (see Davies, 2002). This is not, however, a convincing reason for institutionalising the listing process within a statutory body. Given the absence of any clear rationale for the Official List, the authors would like to see it cease.

The UKLA must ensure that its regulations for listed companies satisfy the requirements of European Union Directives. The UKLA's requirements can and do go beyond those of the EU. To continue on the Official List, companies have to meet various requirements, including publishing accounts and half-yearly reports and making public any material developments in its business that are not public knowledge and which may lead to a substantial movement in its share price.

---

2   http://www.fsa.gov.uk/pubs/annual/ar08_09/ar08_09.pdf.

The FSA is able to fine individuals who break its listing rules or can suspend the listing of shares. Certain offences are also punishable under the criminal law and can lead to a prison sentence (for example, offering shares to the public before a prospectus is issued). Court actions can be launched by the FSA to gain compensation for those parties who may have lost financially as a result of breaches of listing rules.

The FSA has recently adopted 'Listing Principles' as well as listing rules. Three examples of these principles are:

- An issuer must take reasonable steps to enable its directors to understand their responsibilities and obligations as directors.
- An issuer must ensure that it treats all holders of its listed equity securities that are in the same position equally in respect of the rights attaching to such listed equity securities.
- An issuer must deal with the FSA in an open and cooperative manner.

The FSA states that the principles will be interpreted in an 'everyday' rather than a legalistic manner (FSA, 2004). Nevertheless, their purpose is to provide the regulator with more discretion in disciplining firms, as it can now discipline firms for breaking the spirit of the principles as well as for breaking the letter of the rules. Indeed, the whole process is gradually becoming more bureaucratic. There are now 93 subsections in the listing rules section of the FSA handbook, each one of which has a number of provisions. This excludes the sections on prospectus, disclosure and transparency rules.[3]

---

3 See: http://fsahandbook.info/FSA/html/handbook/LR/19/4.

Distinction between listing and trading

The LSE is a private body and has rules that companies must abide by before their shares can be traded on the exchange. To have its shares traded on the LSE a company's main market shares must be on the Official List. This means that the UKLA's listing rules must first be satisfied by the company, as well as the additional requirements set by the LSE. Competing exchanges can develop rules for trading that are appropriate given the constituency of companies that they are trying to attract and their potential investor markets.

In fact, a company does not have to be on the Official List to have its shares traded on a Recognised Investment Exchange (RIE), even though the LSE main market has this as a requirement. Thus, it seems, siting the regulation of the Official List within the regulator is wholly unnecessary. All exchanges, of course, have to ensure that companies whose shares are traded meet FSA requirements relating to conduct of business. Furthermore, the EU requires that companies whose shares are not on the Official List but which are still traded on an exchange meet the requirements of its Prospectus Directive unless they are specifically exempt. This development undermines competition in listing and trading rules substantially and is discussed below. There are now four sources of regulation (the EU, FSA Listing Rules, other FSA rules that apply to all shares, and exchanges) which individually are complex and together overlap to create a framework that is incomprehensible to all but the most highly trained (and expensive) lawyers.

Regulation and the London Stock Exchange

As an RIE, the London Stock Exchange (LSE) has responsibilities to ensure that the operation of each of its markets is orderly, provides proper protection to investors, and promotes and maintains high standards of integrity and fair dealing.

The LSE fulfils these responsibilities in a number of ways, including:

- vetting new applicants for membership;
- monitoring and enforcing members' compliance with its rules;
- monitoring trading on the markets;
- providing services to aid trading;
- conducting preliminary investigations into cases of insider dealing and market abuse.

RIEs are answerable to the FSA. The FSA monitors exchange transactions for signs of 'market abuse' (for example, investigates possibilities of price manipulation when trading is thin). The FSA has extremely wide powers to impose penalties on those found guilty of market abuse. Market abuse is formally defined as misusing information, creating a false or misleading impression, or creating a market distortion.

The LSE's own role in regulating market conduct is discussed in its publication 'Rules of the London Stock Exchange'.[4] Specifically, the LSE states in its preamble that:

> The attractiveness of the Exchange's markets is maintained by providing an efficient and well regulated market place

---

4   http://www.londonstockexchange.com/traders-and-brokers/rules-regula-tions/rules-lse-2009.pdf.

... Orderly markets are maintained via rules, guidance and
through the monitoring of trading and market activity
... The Exchange's primary aim is to provide issuers,
intermediaries and investors with attractive, efficient and
well-regulated markets in which to raise capital and fulfil
investment and trading requirements.

The LSE rule book describes the minutiae of the particular
way in which securities should be traded, etc. When the FSA
developed its Code of Market Conduct (see below), there was
some discussion of whether the exchanges themselves could
provide a 'safe harbour'. Until the creation of the FSA, regulating
conduct has traditionally been the role of independent exchanges,
and they have sophisticated rule books. It was felt by some that
the safe harbour concept, whereby those who obeyed the rules of
the exchange were assumed to have obeyed the rules of the FSA,
would prevent unnecessary duplication of regulation and confusion arising from the duplication of regulatory functions. It was
decided, however, not to grant such status, so FSA regulations are
relevant for dealing in all shares quoted on RIEs at all times, in all
circumstances.

The ability of exchanges to regulate markets is shown by a long
history but also by recent events. The FSA regularly levies fines
for breaking its rules, but exchanges themselves are quite capable
of performing this function in the areas that remain with them or
where there are overlapping competences. Indeed, one recent case
is particularly interesting. In November 2009, AIM fined Regal
(an oil company) for issuing a series of misleading statements to
the market about oil reserves. This is what one would hope an
exchange would do – the exchange wishes to protect its reputation as a reliable place for investors to do business not only by

Box 1 **Exchanges can regulate markets**
The London Stock Exchange, in a document discussing the implementation of the EU Markets in Financial Instruments Directive (MiFID) (London Stock Exchange, 2006), states: 'The London Stock Exchange's commitment to providing a trusted infrastructure for fair and transparent trading and competitive execution is long established.'

The role of the exchange
Whether conducted on or off book, all business is monitored and published by the Exchange and benefits from:

- A reliable and transparent trading environment providing best execution.
- A well-regulated environment that publishes accurate price and trade information in real time.
- Post-trade transparency of off-book trades enabling investors to benchmark performance.
- A highly reliable and fast trading platform enabling efficient trade execution.
- A dedicated supervision team which ensures data integrity via real-time monitoring.
- Competitively priced trade reporting fees.

As well as a centralised and well-regulated market, the Exchange is also able to provide investors with significant protections as a result of its stringent rules. These rules cover:

- Terms of contract between trading counterparts.
- Transparency.

- Administrations of default procedures in the event of member failure.
- Enforcement of settlement rules.
- Structure for the market-making system.

It is very clear that the London Stock Exchange is competing on the basis of the regulation, transparency, efficiency and security that it offers those transacting investments. There is no reason why many of the most important functions that have been given to statutory regulators cannot be returned to exchanges so that they compete with each other and with unregulated trading environments.

imposing rules on investors but also by imposing rules on companies whose shares are traded on the exchange. AIM described the case as unprecedented in terms of the seriousness and in terms of the market impact. It is interesting not only that AIM – a relatively lightly regulated market – did take action, but also that the FSA decided not to take action.[5]

Authorisation of firms to do investment business

Banks can be authorised to carry on a wide range of business in the EU, including investment and securities dealing as well as traditional retail and wholesale banking functions. Investment services firms can be authorised for a narrower range of business

---

5   See: http://www.kattenlaw.co.uk/london/publications/detail.aspx?pub=2518 and http://www.telegraph.co.uk/finance/newsbysector/energy/6592431/FSA-red-faced-as-LSE-fines-Regal.html.

than a bank would be authorised to conduct. This would include: receiving and transmitting orders; dealing as principal or agent; managing portfolios; and underwriting or placing any type of transferable securities, money market instruments or derivatives. Effectively, authorisation is granted to conduct securities business (trading, broking, market-making, etc.) on authorised exchanges. Authorisation also covers the related custody services and so on.

All firms must be authorised to carry on any regulated activity. The conditions for authorisation include any laid down by EU Directives. To obtain permission to carry out regulated activities an organisation must meet certain qualifying conditions. These include having adequate resources (financial resources as well as internal systems and procedures). The conditions are laid out in the FSA's Integrated Handbook. Once permission is granted, authorisation is implicit. The permission can, in effect, be tailor-made so that the FSA can state precisely what activities each firm can be involved with and to what extent. Regulation is bureau-cratic in the extreme. It is no longer possible to determine the number of pages in the handbook, but an indication is given by the following example. There are ten main sections in the book. One of those main sections, relevant to this monograph, is that on 'Listing, prospectus and disclosure'. This contains three subsections which have between nine and 23 sub-subsections each. Taking one of those sub-subsections, under the 'Listing rules', there are six sub-sub-subsections.[6] Those who believe in the lump of labour fallacy will be celebrating the impact on the employment of lawyers!

---

6   See: http://fsahandbook.info/FSA/html/handbook/ (accessed 28 January 2010).

The FSA and investment services company employees

The FSA also has significant control over the authorisation of individuals to perform specific 'controlled' functions. Those functions include senior management functions, where an individual has significant control over regulated activities; those dealing with customers in the conduct of its regulated activities; and those dealing with the property of customers. Thus the FSA has, as part of its remit, the approval of large numbers of senior and possibly not-so-senior staff. The FSA has three months to consider an application for approval and has to establish that the person is a 'fit and proper' person to carry out the relevant function. A number of concerns have been established regarding this function. It vests power in one statutory organisation to determine whether individuals can follow their chosen career; delays could cause serious problems in small firms; and it is not clear why such a function should have to be carried out by a statutory body when the activities that the individuals carry out are themselves regulated by law and statutory regulation. The FSA takes into account honesty, reputation, competence and financial soundness when making the judgement as to whether to authorise individuals. As well as authorisation, the FSA takes a great interest in the training and competence of individuals. In the past this function would have been left to firms, professional bodies and exchanges.

Conclusion

We can be in no doubt about the extensive nature of the FSA. It is not just filling in the gaps or providing an incisive approach to regulation in one or two areas where there is potential for catastrophic market failure. The FSA controls every aspect of the regulation of investment services and the work of investment companies and their employees – it merely delegates some of the less important functions to tightly controlled exchanges.

6 THE FSA, REGULATION AND STATUTORY LAW

Regulation of the conduct of business and market abuse

The FSA has wide powers in relation to the conduct of investment business. The FSA's conduct-of-business rules work alongside the existing criminal law and the rules of individual exchanges.

The FSA's powers to deal with market abuse are very wide-ranging. Unlimited fines can be imposed on all individuals, whether or not they are authorised, who engage in market abuse. The breadth of the FSA's powers in this regard is controversial. Market abuse involves behaviour which is of a standard that a regular user of the market would regard as inadequate and it has to involve qualifying investments on registered exchanges (not direct property, for example). Market abuse includes providing misleading information, manipulating the market or trading with inside information.

There are three main elements to the market abuse regime (see FSA, 2000). The first is the use of insider information, described by the FSA as the 'misuse of information'. The second is behaviour that gives a false or misleading impression to investors about the price of, supply of or demand for a particular security. The third is behaviour that 'distorts' the market. Looking at the issue slightly differently, we can say that market abuse tends to fall into two categories. The first category is action taken to distort price signals.

When price signals are distorted they convey inaccurate information. They thus both undermine market efficiency and also give an advantage to the investor who has distorted the signals (who may buy or sell securities at distorted prices while knowing their underlying value). The second category involves dealing when privy to information that is not generally known in the market.

The FSA regulates market conduct on registered investment exchanges through a 'Code of Market Conduct'. This is an important mechanism by which the FSA tries to define what is meant by 'market abuse'. The aim of the code is set out by the FSA: 'Through its descriptions of what is and what is not acceptable, the Code sets out in more detail the standards that should be observed by everybody who uses the UK markets.'[1] The code is described as 'good news for retail investors' because it will make it more difficult for others to take advantage of any information that has not yet been made available to all investors. It is designed to ensure that prices are not manipulated to the disadvantage of some investors. It was under this code that restrictions on short selling were brought in during the banking crisis.

In economic terms, market abuse often involves distorting price signals so that they no longer fulfill their proper role of conveying information to buyers and sellers. As such, traders engaged in such abuse may be able to gain from trading in a share where they know that prices have been distorted. Encouraging or requiring others to engage in market abuse is regarded just as seriously as engaging in it oneself. There are some cases where market manipulation or abuse could be regarded as criminal activities as they represent, in effect, attempts to defraud people

---

1   FSA Factsheet, 'Why market abuse could cost you money', December 2001.

of their property. For example, if providing misleading information causes individuals to buy shares at a higher price than they otherwise would have done, then people are, in effect, deprived of money that is legitimately their own – even if the provision of misleading information were to the market as a whole, rather than to specific individuals. Such an offence is similar to 'clocking' a car. Indeed, the criminal law does still address these matters (see below).

The purpose of the Code of Market Conduct is to provide a flexible framework that enables the FSA to state what may or may not be regarded as market abuse. Also, if the Code suggested that a particular form of behaviour was not market abuse, then this would be regarded as acceptable evidence that market abuse had not been committed.

Conflicts of interest

The potential for conflicts of interest has long been a concern for lawmakers and financial regulators. Indeed, the 1934 Glass-Steagall Act in the USA, which determined the shape of the US banking system for decades, was a response to the perceived problem of conflicts of interest within banks. At the root of the perceived problem is the cost of collecting valuable investment information. This leads to synergies between different investment activities and in the provision of different investment products. A balanced discussion of the problem of conflicts of interest in the provision of investment services can be found in Chapter 2 of Crockett et al. (2003). Two examples, relating to the provision of investment research, are worthy of note. If an investment bank is involved in both underwriting and the provision of investment

Box 2 **Mind your own business!**

The muddle that we can get into by handing over the regulation of private investment market transactions to statutory regulators can be seen by the recent move by the Treasury and the FSA to explore the rules for conducting rights issues.[1]

At the same time, the FSA was deciding how to regulate short sales. Yet it is the regulation of rights issues – which lengthens the rights issue process – which is a major factor in exposing companies to the problems of short selling. The Treasury and the FSA were examining whether to allow companies to issue more shares without a general meeting, thus more than halving the timetable necessary for a rights issue. They were also considering other options, such as an option to make a rights issue in specific circumstances without seeking the approval of shareholders, a reduction in the period available for shareholders to take their rights and a simplification of the prospectus procedures.

It is difficult to imagine a subject less appropriate for statutory regulation. What has it got to do with the Treasury? It is quite conceivable that different companies in different situations would approach the problem in different ways. Those who suffer from the wrong procedures being followed are shareholders – and most shares are held by large investing institutions. The company itself could determine the processes and these could form part of its Articles of Association. The main exchange on which the company was traded could be responsible for developing further appropriate rules if necessary – after all, it has an incentive to keep both potential buyers and

---

1   See *Daily Telegraph*, 28 July 2008.

sellers of shares and the listing company happy. The market has institutions that are capable of resolving these problems.

research, it may have an incentive to provide biased research so that the price of the share is boosted during the underwriting period. Similarly, if the investment bank is involved in both trading and investment research, it may have an incentive to provide research that encourages purchases of a share if the bank is long in the share on its trading book. There are many other possible examples of conflicts of interest. The FSA notes (FSA, 2002), for example, that the proportion of 'buy' recommendations made by firms acting as corporate brokers or advisers to the company about whom the recommendation is being made is, at 80 per cent, twice as high as the proportion of 'buy' recommendations where the analyst does not work for the corporate broker.

The existence of conflicts of interest does not, in itself, justify regulation. Market participants can judge whether to obtain research from an organisation that carries out research alone (with, presumably, higher costs) or from an investment bank that obtains synergies from the provision of an array of services.

The FSA regulates conflicts of interest through many aspects of its regime, including the Code of Market Conduct and the Listing Rules. Various ways of managing conflicts of interest are regarded as acceptable. These would include: maintaining internal arrangements that prevent the flow of information within the firm (a Chinese wall); disclosing an interest to the customer; or having a policy of independence and declining to act for a customer if there is a conflict of interest. Firms that publish objective research must set out a policy explaining how they identify and manage conflicts of interest and thus ensure their clients' impartiality. There are also restrictions on firms dealing before investment research has been published. In the chapters below we argue that this type of regulation does not have to be provided by a statutory body.

The criminal law and financial regulation

There is existing criminal law dealing with wrongdoing in financial markets, such as making misleading statements, market manipulation and insider dealing. Successful prosecution under these laws can bring a jail sentence of seven years. These offences remain criminal offences and the FSA can bring prosecutions against anybody under the criminal codes.

The first of these criminal activities is concerned with those who make misleading or false or deceptive statements or conceal material facts that could lead somebody to make investment decisions they otherwise would not have made. This crime can take place in a number of contexts – including providing false information in takeover documents, as well as market-makers passing on false research information. Market manipulation also falls under the criminal code. This includes acts that might give the impression that a share is more liquid than it really is or that its price is different from the underlying price (for example, by deliberately purchasing a share in times of illiquid markets in order to cause its traded volume or price to rise).

These kinds of activity would generally seem to be criminal in character in cases where there is a deliberate attempt to defraud by providing misleading information. Issues such as an individual not disclosing information, however, even where there is not a deliberate attempt to mislead by providing false information, should be dealt with by the civil law, or perhaps through private regulatory systems developed by exchanges themselves.

Insider dealing is also a criminal act – though whether it should be is certainly debatable. Insider trading occurs when an individual who is privy to significant information about a company that is not in the public domain (significant in the sense that it would affect the share price) deals or encourages others to deal. An offence also takes place if an individual discloses the information to others who it is expected may deal. A case can certainly be made for not including these activities in the criminal law. Indeed, there are specific FSA market conduct requirements related to the disclosure of information by companies to ensure that such a disclosure is made to all shareholders simultaneously. Again, such market conduct requirements are arguably the province of an exchange.

All these criminal activities are also outlawed by the FSA's Code of Market Conduct, for which a civil degree of proof is required and which is not enforced through the normal courts but in the FSA's own tribunals. It was felt that it was too difficult to successfully bring criminal prosecutions for these activities and that their inclusion in the FSA's Code of Market Conduct would help enforcement.

Thus the FSA Code of Market Conduct is designed to cover a wider range of activities than can be covered by the criminal law. Although the degree of proof that is required to find a person guilty of an offence by the FSA is less than that in a criminal court, the penalties the FSA can impose are harsh, including unlimited financial penalties. The Code covers anybody who may deal on markets regardless of whether they are registered or not; it covers all prescribed markets whether regulated or not; and it even covers activity in the relevant investments which is 'off exchange' (for example, spread betting in a share quoted on AIM).

Although exchanges have had most of their functions super-seded by statutory bodies, they can make supplementary rules. There are also rules on takeovers and acquisitions developed by the Takeover Panel. The FSA can apply such rules as if they were FSA rules, if it wishes. The FSA can also make rules relating to the internal structures of stock exchange firms. For example, as noted above, they can require the creation of 'Chinese walls' restricting the circulation of information within a firm.

Disciplining of individuals and firms

Approved individuals or firms may be disciplined by the FSA if they knowingly break its rules. Individuals are also required, however, to abide by a statement of principles. The statement of principles requires individuals to behave with integrity; due skill, care and diligence; observe proper standards of market conduct; and so on.

There are two main functions of the FSA in relation to discipline and enforcement. These are sometimes described (see Alcock, 2000) as 'policing the perimeter' and 'disciplining author-ised firms and individuals'. In everyday language, this could be described as making sure that only authorised firms and individuals do business and ensuring that those that are authorised abide by the rules. It is a bit like the distinction between policing the borders of a country to prevent illegal immigration and policing the country itself to make sure its citizens behave.

In relation to policing the perimeter, if an unauthorised

person performs a function that requires authorisation or makes false claims that they are authorised, criminal proceedings can be instituted by the FSA. In addition, civil action can also be taken against such people for damages, to obtain injunctions and to institute bankruptcy proceedings.

The FSA has wide disciplinary powers in relation to authorised firms and individuals. As well as using its own mechanisms, the FSA can bring prosecutions against authorised firms and approved individuals under the FSMA 2000, and also under other legislation that it has already been noted exists to deal with market conduct and criminal activity (for example, money laundering and insider-dealing legislation).

When using its own disciplinary procedures against firms, the FSA can carry out a public reprimand, levy a fine, impose orders for damages, cancel permission to carry out certain regulated activity or withdraw authorisation. The FSA can also take disciplinary action against individuals. The FSA tribunal can determine its own burden of proof.

Unreasonable powers

These powers do give rise to some serious philosophical questions. Apart from sending somebody to prison, the FSA can do almost anything that a criminal court can do, yet its burden of proof and integrity of process is not the same. The FSA can bankrupt an individual or firm and it can prevent an individual or firm from following their profession or chosen line of business. The FSA has three features that, in combination, are of serious concern. It has a statutory monopoly of regulatory services: if the FSA withdraws authorisation it is not possible to practise one's profession in financial markets; the FSA has criminal powers of punishment; yet, despite this, the FSA has the same standards of proof and procedure that one would expect of a voluntary private body.

It is helpful in this context to distinguish between government and private regulation. Criminal and civil law require a certain degree of proof and adherence to procedure. Such law is made by Parliament but enforced by the courts. Specific government law, as we have seen, already exists in relation to financial services. Private regulation, on the other hand, is laid down by private organisations, membership of which is voluntary. Such private organisations administer their own punishments and develop their own procedures, and those who enter the private body accept its discipline. Examples include the Football Association, which is regularly in the news when it invokes its disciplinary procedures, professional bodies and stock exchanges. Private entities are the right vehicles for providing regulation, which naturally has to adapt to changing conditions. The appropriate domain of the state is the provision of law, which should be broadly defined, stable and interpreted by the courts.

Before 1988 financial regulation fell clearly into one of these two categories of criminal or civil law and regulation. Each system had its own checks and balances and constraints. The current body of financial regulation and the powers it gives to the FSA have none of the constraints of either the private system of regulation or the government system of law, yet broadly have the power of the government system of law. It could be argued that they fall outside the 'rule of law': that is, FSA regulation and procedures are not governed by the principles that we would normally expect to govern the law. Indeed, once again, it should be noted that some of the offences against which the FSA can take action are in fact criminal offences and could be dealt with under the due process of government law.

An additional problem of the current approach to financial regulation is the sheer difficulty of obeying the rules. On the one hand, some aspects of rules that have to be followed by individuals and firms are so detailed they may be difficult to understand. On the other hand, some rules are very general, and individuals and firms will not necessarily know how the FSA is to interpret them.

Should there be one regulator or many?

There are other bodies that have made rules and regulations about conduct of business, listing, trading and so on in UK financial markets. Indeed, since the development of sophisticated financial markets in the nineteenth century, investment market conduct has been governed by the common law, the criminal law, the civil law, contract law, rules developed by exchanges and professions and other ad hoc bodies that have been set up or which have evolved in the market from time to time. The FSA now deals with nearly all aspects of financial regulation, including some aspects that might be regarded as criminal issues.

It may be thought that it is more efficient or effective to have a single financial regulator. It may be the case, however, that, as in other aspects of commercial activity, different forms of law-making and rule-making may be necessary in different contexts and that it is necessary to have different levels of rule-making bodies – as well as competition. For example, the criminal law code could deal with issues of fraud; the civil law with misrepresentation; market exchanges with market conduct issues such as price manipulation; and so on.

The FSMA (2000) gives power to the FSA to deal with issues such as insider dealing, market manipulation and providing false information while maintaining the existing criminal statutes. This gives the impression that legislators cannot determine whether particular aspects of regulation should, in principle, be criminal or civil offences or left to private regulation, so all options are left open. If an offence cannot be proven to criminal levels of proof, the FSA can take action and impose an unlimited fine. On the other hand, the possibility of criminal action still remains, potentially leading to even stiffer penalties: this is surely an abuse of power.

Rules relating to conduct of business are necessarily highly complex and it is legitimate to ask whether it is reasonable, or indeed possible, to require a statutory regulator to develop the complex web of rules (or indeed, exercise restraint in rule-making where restraint is appropriate) that is necessary in investment markets. In the past, rules would have been developed by exchanges which were specific and intended to deal with the particular types of transaction that took place on the exchange. The optimal rules cannot be determined except by a process of competition between exchanges whose role is to provide orderly markets and develop rules that will maximise the value of exchange services to members. This is a convincing argument for a return to regulatory competition between private bodies (see below). If there are additional areas of interest for the civil and criminal law codes or, for that matter, for the common law, that should be a matter for Parliament and the courts.

The same arguments relate to the rules governing the

behaviour of individuals. Individual exchanges and professions – as well as companies – can develop their own rules for determining whether individuals can work in different capacities. Indeed, such systems already work alongside the FSA systems, though they are rapidly becoming subservient to it. Before statutory regulation, there was a long history of private regulation and disciplining of individuals – indeed, as has been noted, this applied from the origin of the London exchange. Clearly, the criminal law can apply and there is no reason why the state should not facilitate the checking of whether an individual has committed particular criminal offences on behalf of a profession or exchange. FSA regulation and licensing, however, make the acquisition of a reputation for hiring well-qualified and reputable staff less valuable for firms and undermine the roles of trade bodies and professions in ensuring that staff in appropriate roles are suitably qualified.

7 CURRENT DEVELOPMENTS AND THE ROLE OF THE EUROPEAN UNION

Approaches to the development of EU regulation

There are two basic approaches to the development of regulation at EU level. The first involves harmonisation of all EU regulation at the same level. This approach has been rejected, at least in principle, for wholesale investment markets. The second approach involves harmonisation of some common standards and a process of mutual recognition whereby institutions that fulfil the regulatory requirements of one EU country are assumed to fulfil the requirements of all EU countries. It is worth noting that there is an alternative to 'harmonisation' and 'mutual recognition' – liberalisation.

Different countries take different views on the extent of regulation that they regard as necessary at state level and thus the mutual recognition approach is sometimes regarded as a compromise between harmonisation and liberalisation. Harmonised minimum standards can also put limits on the extent of regulation that countries can develop under the mutual recognition procedure. They can, therefore, lead to liberalisation in many EU countries.

Under the Lamfalussy initiative described below, the basic approach to the development of EU regulation for the issue of securities has been to develop some core principles by which harmonised regulations are formulated. These form the basis of a 'common passport' which can be used to issue and trade securities under the regulatory framework in any EU country. National markets can build further regulations on top of the core harmonised requirements. The principles for the authorisation of investment services firms are similar: if the requirements for authorisation are met in any one EU country, than an investment firm is deemed to be authorised to do business in all EU countries.

A number of EU regulations and Directives[1] were brought in under single market regulation. Owing to concern about the slow speed with which the single market programme was developing in the financial services sector, however, the European Commission published a Communication containing a Financial Services Action Plan (FSAP) that was designed to fill gaps in the single market process by 2005. Both regulations and Directives were used to implement FSAP and the process took somewhat longer than anticipated (see HM Treasury et al., 2003, for a user-friendly guide to FSAP, and FSA, 2005a).

The main EU initiatives were: a Market Abuse Directive (more or less implemented by 2005); a Prospectus Directive (2005); a revised Investment Services Directive known as the Markets in Financial Instrument Directive or MiFID (2007); a Transparency Directive (2007); and regulation relating to accounting disclosures which requires listed companies to use international accounting standards (effectively fair value accounting methods) for reporting purposes (2005).

Because of the technical difficulty of many of these measures the 'Lamfalussy process' was developed whereby framework

---

1   Directives require implementation action by member states; regulations are im-
    plemented directly in all member states.

legislation is proposed by the Commission and European Parliament and then detailed regulation is developed and implemented by special committees with reference back to the European Parliament. There are also complementary measures and proposals to develop a minimum framework of EU law for the approval of takeovers and the protection of shareholders in takeovers.

Broadly, all these EU measures can be divided into two groups: those that deal with information provision by companies to investors and those that deal with market conduct.

The regulation of information provision
Accounting standards

There are three aspects of EU regulation on information provision by companies to the market – the Prospectus Directive, the Transparency Directive and the implementation of International Accounting Standards (IAS).

The issues surrounding the imposition of compulsory, uniform, detailed accounting standards are discussed in Myddelton (2004) and we broadly agree with Myddelton's conclusions that imposition of standards by statutory bodies is neither necessary nor desirable. We therefore just make brief comment here. It is not at all clear why very specific methods of accounting are an issue for regulation. There is no consensus about the best methods, and to enshrine particular detailed methods in regulation across the whole of the EU must undermine the evolution of better approaches. Standards for the provision of accounting information can be determined at many levels: by individual professionals, by professional bodies, by stock exchanges, by national law and by EU law. We would argue that professions, as well as exchanges, have an incentive to develop appropriate standards and that this does not need to be a function of a transnational body. Indeed, the Committee of European Securities Regulators (CESR, 2003) has stated, 'the transition [to IAS] must be carefully monitored by regulators to ensure ... that investors are able to understand the effect of the new reporting standards on the financial position of listed companies'. Ensuring that investors understand accounting information in the companies in which they have chosen to invest is surely well outside the role and competence of a regulator. In short, these directives reduce regulatory competition and impose a single way of providing information.

The Prospectus Directive[2]

The EU Prospectus Directive requires companies to produce a prospectus when they offer securities for sale to the public or admit their securities for trading on a regulated market. The prospectus has to be approved by the relevant authorities (the FSA in the UK). The Prospectus Directive is discussed in full in HM Treasury and FSA (2004) and issues related to its implementation by the FSA are discussed in FSA (2004). The pre-existing legislative framework for listed securities remained in place even after the Prospectus Directive was implemented. This has a number of ramifications. For example, the FSA is able to impose rules that go beyond the Prospectus Directive for companies on its Official List. It cannot prevent a company making a public offer under the terms of the Directive, however, or trading its shares on

---

2   There is currently an amendment to the Prospectus Directive being discussed which, among other changes, suggests making companies liable for decisions taken by investors on the basis of brief prospectus summary documents.

a regulated market, subject to the regulations of the market, if the company fulfils the terms of the Prospectus Directive in the UK or elsewhere.

Once a company has had its prospectus accepted by the relevant authorities in one EU member state, it becomes valid in other EU member states, so that its securities can be traded on regulated markets or offered to the public throughout the EU. A company will not, however, necessarily satisfy the requirements for a listing in other member states if those other member states exercise their right to impose further regulations on listed securities within their jurisdiction. In addition, individual exchanges can have trading requirements regardless of whether a company is listed. All very confusing ...

The definition of a public offer that comes within the remit of the Directive is very wide. There are various exemptions, however, which allow companies in particular situations not to issue a prospectus complying with the Directive. These include situations where offers of securities are addressed to a small number of investors or only to 'qualified investors' (see HM Treasury and FSA (2004) for a description of the exemptions and definition of qualified investors). In addition, a public offer below €2.5 million is outside the scope of the Directive. Securities that are exempt from the Directive at the time of an initial offer come under the Directive if they are not exempt at the time of any resale. Those companies whose securities are traded on a regulated market are required to provide an annual document containing or referring to all information that they have published or made available to the public over the previous twelve months.

Statutory rules about prospectuses are completely unnecessary. One of the purposes of exchanges is to establish such rules

– as the London Stock Exchange did very effectively. Appropriate rules may change from time to time and may be different for different types of company. Statutory regulation across the EU simply impedes competition – and may fossilise existing practice.

Transparency Directive

The Transparency Directive establishes rules on periodic financial reports and on disclosure of major shareholdings for issuers whose securities are admitted for trading on a regulated market. Specifically, the Directive requires the following:

- All issuers of shares and debt securities must produce annual and half-yearly reports. Issuers of shares must produce interim management statements.
- Holders of shares must notify the market when their levels of holdings move above certain thresholds.
- Shareholder meetings and changes to the terms and conditions of an issue must be notified according to certain procedures.
- All information that is disclosed under the Directive (and some information disclosed under the Market Abuse Directive) must be disseminated on an EU-wide basis and stored centrally. Member states must also establish guidelines to ensure public access to this information.

According to the FSA (2005b: 17), the Transparency Directive 'requires a high standard of continuous [*sic*] reporting by companies, enabling shareholders to make informed investment decisions'. It is unclear why such regulation cannot be determined by stock exchanges – including stock exchanges that operate on a pan-EU basis. The Directive has now been implemented and the FSA is also free to add extra requirements in addition to those required by the Directive.

The Transparency Directive also covers matters traditionally determined by the Takeover Panel in the UK. These include the notification of when shareholdings go beyond a particular threshold. The current rules in the UK are, in fact, less liberal than the proposed minimum standards to be implemented across the EU. It is possible that the UK will, in fact, liberalise its rules when the Directive is implemented.

The provision of investment services and the regulation of market conduct and abuse
Markets in Financial Instruments Directive (MiFID)

MiFID was implemented during 2007. It replaced the Investment Services Directive. MiFID regulates the authorisation and conduct of securities firms and markets. The Directive required significant changes to the FSA's Conduct of Business Sourcebook (FSA, 2005a). The Directive affects not just authorisation but management of conflicts of interest, financial promotions, standards for exchanges, transparency obligations and so on.

One of the main purposes of MiFID is to promote cross-border provision of investment services. It specifies, at an EU level, the types of investment instruments and services that need authorisation from an appropriate authority. If a firm has authorisation from one EU member country, it can operate in any member country. One of the objectives of the Directive is to facilitate competition across different forms of trading platforms in different member states. MiFID will regulate the operation of multilateral trading facilities and over-the-counter markets that compete with existing exchanges. It will also regulate investment banks that settle trades within their own book in the same way as exchanges are regulated.[3] Thus the MiFID regulations will apply to banks that undertake trades by matching buying and selling orders from their own clients' orders and which therefore act in effect as private exchanges. Firms trading on behalf of clients will have to meet new standards of price transparency both before and after trades. Firms will have to report transactions, whether on or off exchange. Derivatives fall under the remit of the directive too.

MiFID also expands the definition of 'best execution' of orders on behalf of clients. A wide-ranging definition is used that goes beyond the achievement of the best price available for clients. Macey and O'Hara (2005) criticise this approach to regulation in the USA. They point out that the requirement of an agent to work in the best interests of a principal is a fundamental principle of common law and that developing detailed regulations to ensure that this is achieved is not possible. It is worth noting that conflicts of interest with regard to best execution were exacerbated in UK financial markets as a result of the Office of Fair Trading investigation into the London Stock Exchange and the subsequent market reforms discussed above.

Like the Prospectus Directive, MiFID therefore undermines competition in the provision of regulatory services as those who wish to use multilateral trading facilities or over-the-counter

3   For example, Goldman Sachs may have one client selling 1,000,000 BT shares and two clients buying 600,000 each. Goldman Sachs can use the sales to provide most of the shares for the purchasers without trading through an exchange. Such transactions will become heavily regulated. The process is known as 'systematic internalisation' in MiFID.

methods of trading will not be able to choose to expose themselves to a different regulatory environment. The requirement to reveal prices at which trades take place, so that data is not fragmented across competing trading platforms, seems unnecessary. There is no reason why commercial firms cannot provide the function of collecting and publicising price information; this is precisely how information was compiled historically in the London Stock Exchange: the *Financial Times* had a commercial interest in collecting information. While the EU's fears that information might become segmented could be realised, with adverse consequences for the market, it would seem reasonable to react to an actual 'market failure' rather than institutionalise the market failure. It is felt by the EU that there is a risk that market participants would have an incomplete picture of the UK marketplace and would find it more difficult to identify the best price, thus undermining the efficiency of the market, if participants were not required to report trades (see London Stock Exchange, 2006). This seems to negate one of the fundamental functions of intermediaries, which is to specialise in the collection and assimilation of price information.

Overall, MiFID could probably best be described as an attempt to create competition between 'state-designed' markets. This is a fundamental error – the process of competition is necessary to find the best market design just as the process of competition is necessary between operators within similar markets. In its favour, MiFID will significantly reduce regulation of many EU markets, thus facilitating a limited form of competition between existing exchanges. MiFID should not be seen wholly as an attempt to increase regulation, even if that is its effect in some countries.

Market Abuse Directive

A Market Abuse Directive was implemented in 2005. This created an EU-wide regime covering insider trading and market manipulation. The Directive also provides a common framework for the disclosure of market-sensitive information as a protection against insider dealing. For example, it is prohibited to start or spread misleading rumours; and information must be made public in a manner that enables fast access and complete, correct and timely assessment by the public. The Directive requires that conflicts of interest should be disclosed when presenting research or recommendations. Furthermore, all companies have to draw up lists of people who *might* have inside information – something that has been deemed an impossible task.

It is explicit in the Directive that a single regulatory authority should be responsible in each member state. In other words, regulatory competition is effectively prohibited. The FSA have implemented the new EU Directive fully while maintaining the requirements of the existing FSA regime. In other words, where the existing regime is wider than the Directive, the existing regime will be maintained; where the Directive is wider, it will be implemented.

An assessment of the EU agenda

The arguments for and against statutory regulation of investment markets are discussed below. It is worth making some specific points on the EU agenda at this stage, however.

Where there is a genuine mutual recognition approach, competition between regulators may be facilitated. A company, for example, could trade its securities across a range of markets while falling under the jurisdiction of any chosen state regulator. If a particular regulator had the wrong balance of regulatory rules, a company could list under a different regime and still have its shares traded across the EU. Unfortunately, there is a substantial amount of harmonised regulation (MiFID is the most notable example).[4] Thus, rather than promoting regulatory competition, the EU agenda is, in practice, creating greater uniformity and a higher level of regulation across the EU. Also, under MiFID, the EU is undermining dynamic competition between different forms of investment market that have different regulations. All methods of transacting investments, whether through an exchange or not, will be subject to the same framework of regulation. This will not only raise costs and undermine the discovery of new approaches to regulating markets; it will also prevent market innovation. Finally, it is worth noting that many particular EU regulations require an FSA-style monopoly regulatory authority in each country.

---

4   There are occasions where the EU has harmonised regulation in ways that prohibit countries from developing particular types of regulation – including in the
area covered by this monograph. For example, MiFID prevents countries from
requiring domestic equities to be traded on domestic exchanges. Whenever
the EU harmonises some minimum level of regulation, however, it is effectively
creating a monopoly and preventing regulatory competition.

8 THE ECONOMIC CASE FOR GOVERNMENT REGULATION EXAMINED

Introduction

An economic case can be constructed for the regulation of investment activity such as that which takes place through stock exchanges. Regulation can be justified because of the potential for externalities where the behaviour of parties on the exchange affects other parties (for example, poor behaviour by an individual or firm can raise suspicions about other individuals or firms). As in all other activities involving purchases and sales, there is also the potential for information asymmetries between clients and firms and for investors to 'abuse' markets by trading in 'thin' markets in a way that intentionally distorts price signals.

In theory, these problems can be overcome by regulation, although whether they should be overcome by *government* regulation or can be overcome in practice are different matters. Therefore, to accept that there is a case for regulation is not to accept that there is a case for such regulation to come from statutory bodies. If externalities are contained within parties that operate on the exchange, there is an incentive for the exchange to develop mechanisms to resolve the problems. Market mechanisms may therefore evolve to deal with problems that are today dealt with by statutory regulators. There may be a case for statutory regulation if there are factors that prevent effective private regulatory bodies evolving[1] or if externalities go beyond those parties that can efficiently contract with each other. But even here, the case for regulation is weakened when one considers the problems highlighted by public choice economics (see Chapter 9).

The next two chapters consider a number of issues that help establish the case for regulation and help provide an indication of the forms of bodies that could and should provide that regulation. Specifically the following issues are considered:

- the economic case for the regulation of investment transactions;
- the prima facie economic case for the failure of market institutions, such as exchanges, to provide the optimal degree of regulation;
- the case for private institutions and the case against government institutions providing such regulation.

In considering public choice economics and the problems of state regulation we look at the 'law of unintended consequences' and the relationship between state regulation and scandals. In looking at the possibilities for private regulation to emerge, we also consider the relationship between 'accountability' and 'trust'.

Llewellyn (1999) produced the first FSA Occasional Paper, discussing the economic rationale for financial regulation. This paper was broader than our own: nevertheless, its arguments are

---

1   These factors could include problems created by the provisions of law in other fields. For example, it is possible that laws relating to the restraint of trade might prevent an exchange from imposing a particular punishment, even if the mechanism that gave rise to that punishment was agreed between the parties. We have already seen that people have tried to use the restraint-of-trade rationale to justify breaking up private exchanges.

useful in providing a framework for discussion. Below we consider some of those arguments.

Externalities from investment transactions

Externalities may arise from the behaviour of firms involved in securities business. The externalities problem is frequently used as a justification for the regulation of the solvency and liquidity position of banks. For example, bank failures can have repercussions for the payments system the effects of which are felt beyond those contracting with the affected bank. It is possible to envisage such problems with regard to investment transactions too. It will suffice to give two examples. Investment transactions often involve the assimilation of a considerable amount of information regarding the probity of the parties involved. Reputation is important because of the costs of analysing information relating to the probity of individual firms. If one firm in a market behaves badly it may damage the reputation of other firms and reduce investor confidence more generally. Thus regulation might help maintain market confidence, which is, in fact, one of the objectives of the FSA. A second example follows from this. Standardisation of contracts, of types of information offered to investors, and so on can reduce transactions costs significantly. If investment contracts are standardised, it will benefit other firms using the same contracts, thus creating a positive externality as firms have to accumulate less information to understand contracts: indeed, standardised contracts might be regarded as a 'club good'.[2]

---

2   We do not root our arguments generally in the club-good literature – though it is implicit. Financial regulation of the sort with which we are concerned in this monograph, however, is generally a club good. That is, regulation provides

Box 3 **Self-regulation versus market regulation**

At different times in different countries, including in the UK before 1986, regulatory functions have been provided by private exchanges. This has been discussed in detail in earlier chapters. That regulatory functions can be performed by private bodies is not in doubt. Indeed, the FSA's own operating arrangements with market exchanges contain phrases such as: 'The Exchanges wish to maintain fair and transparent markets that are attractive to market participants'; and: 'The FSA and the Exchanges recognise that there are areas in which they have an overlapping remit in terms of their functions and powers in relation to market misconduct.' The operating arrangements are designed to prevent multiple investigations of the same matter because it is recognised that the interests of the FSA and those of the exchanges are often the same.

The perceived failure of the period of 'self'-regulation from 1986 to 1997 is often taken as a justification for statutory regulation. Self-regulation as it is commonly understood, however, is quite different from the regulatory forces that spontaneously develop in a market. The so-called self-regulatory systems that have been developed, both by the 1934 Securities and Exchange Act in the USA and the 1986 Financial Services Act in the UK, have been very far from market-based regulatory systems. The defining characteristic of these forms of self-regulation is that a series of 'self-regulatory organisations' were set up that operated under the jurisdiction of a statutory body reporting to a department of government. Such self-regulatory bodies could be regarded as state-created private monopolies accountable to the state. Competition was absent from the process of developing regulation in both cases.

It is worth mentioning that, in the case of the US so-called self-regulatory system, the end result has not been that which was anticipated. The system was originally described by the second Securities and Exchange Commission (SEC) chairman, William O. Douglas, in the following terms: '[T]he exchanges take the leadership with Government playing a residual role. Government would keep that shotgun, so to speak, behind the door, loaded, well-oiled, cleaned and ready for use but with the hope it would never be used' (see Oesterle, 2000). It could be felt that, if this analogy is valid, it creates a tension and imbalance of power between the regulators and those who are regulated which is destructive rather than creative. In any case, by 1975 Congress amended the 1934 Act to require explicit SEC approval of all new rules produced by self-regulatory organisations. The SEC now has the power to write such rules. As Oesterle puts it, the shotgun is not behind the door; rather the finger is on the trigger to ensure that the self-regulatory organisations do what the SEC wishes (ibid.).

We do not consider so-called self-regulation further. It is really a particular form of state regulation. In so far as it has been adjudged to have failed, it is this particular form of state-regulation which has failed, not the market which has failed. The phrase 'self-regulation' is an inappropriate phrase to describe this approach to regulation. Instead we distinguish between state regulation and regulation that evolves through the spontaneous order of market mechanisms. State regulation can take a number of different forms, one of which is the form sometimes referred to as 'self-regulation'.

There is a distinction between the regulation of banks and the regulation of securities markets: the prima facie arguments for banking regulation are much stronger. If a bank reneges on its commitments, any economic agent can be seriously affected – including economic agents who do not contract with the banking system at all. In the case of the regulation of investment transactions, however, it is by no means clear that the externalities significantly affect those who are not party to investment transactions. Thus, in principle, market mechanisms can regulate investment transactions.[3] This could happen, for example, by exchanges developing standardised contracts, regulating information provision and aspects of market conduct. Indeed, the economic gains from the development of standardised information provision and standardised contracts are some of the prime motivating factors for the development of exchanges. It is also important to note that statutory regulation itself is an important source of externalities. The costs of regulation are imposed on parties that do not necessarily benefit from it and, in so far as regulators' responses to the problems that they seek to solve are sub-optimal, they will impose policies the costs of which are greater than the benefits.

Information asymmetries

A second set of problems can arise as a result of 'information asymmetries'. Simply put, these arise where one party to a

---

benefits where there is non-rivalry but from which people can be excluded. The exchanges that traditionally regulated investment markets are a club established for the benefit of those who wish to avail themselves of its regulatory services; members then sell services underpinned by those benefits to clients.

3   The authors believe that market mechanisms could regulate banks too, but we do not pursue that here.

transaction has more information than the other party and the costs of resolving the asymmetry are non-trivial. The potential for information asymmetries in financial markets is considerable. It is this problem which frequently gives rise to the demand for the regulation of both financial product markets and the regulation of non-bank financial institutions such as insurance companies and pensions funds (see, for example Booth, 2003, and Morrison, 2004). No market – financial or otherwise – operates without information asymmetries, however, and there is no limit to the regulation that could be imposed to remove them. Regulation to address information asymmetries could involve disclosure requirements to increase the availability of information or regulation that puts greater responsibility upon those who have the superior information. Financial markets are said to be prone to information asymmetries because information is costly to collect, is complex, subjective and often closely held by a small number of parties. Also, transactions often involve large sums of money changing hands infrequently rather than small sums changing hands frequently.

Information asymmetries are often seen to lead to 'unfairness' between parties to a transaction. In fact, their main economic effect is to reduce the number of contracts written to below the optimal level (see Akerlof, 1970). For example, if parties to a share transaction know that information asymmetries exist they may choose not to buy shares. To use an analogy, imagine a situation where a hill walker in a particular country did not know whether there were landmines in an attractive part of the country. One form of harm coming from this would be that some hill walkers would be blown up. But another, less visible, form of harm would arise from hill walkers deciding not to go walking in the area. It is the same with financial contracts. Harm may come from information asymmetries when those affected lose money, but less visible harm arises because people opt out of the market because of concerns about information asymmetries and concerns that they will be sold a 'lemon'.[4, 5]

There is no question that information asymmetries exist in securities markets and that their impact can be serious. It is certainly not clear, however, that statutory regulators are necessary to deal with the problem. Indeed, in the UK stock market, principal and agent functions were separated for investment transactions on the UK market until 'Big Bang' in 1986 for this reason. An exchange has an incentive to develop regulations regarding information provision to help overcome information asymmetry problems as it makes the exchange more attractive for trading. Such regulations existed on stock exchanges before the Financial Services Act 1986 and still exist today (though statutory regulation increasingly plays an important role). One difficulty, which we discuss below, is that exchanges may not respond to the needs of 'small' investors, who may suffer particularly from the information asymmetry problem and for whom the transactions costs of overcoming information asymmetries are particularly high. Credit rating agencies, however, which help overcome information asymmetries in the bond market, are a good example of where the holders of the information themselves pay the cost of overcoming information asymmetries because the issuer of capital benefits from a lower cost of capital.[6] Indeed, private stock

---

4   To use the second-hand-car terminology of Akerlof (1970).

5   The argument is a little more complex than this, and the landmine analogy is not complete. There can also be a 'race to the bottom' in the presence of information asymmetries.

6   This aspect of credit rating agencies has been criticised by some analysts since the crash of 2008. Different mechanisms will evolve to deal with different situations,

exchanges can be regarded as another example of a vehicle by which issuers of capital overcome information asymmetries: the company pays for a listing and abides by listing rules, because by doing so it will reduce the cost of capital by extending the range of investors who are willing to contract with it.

Insider trading and market abuse
Dealing with insider trading

Insider trading (a criminal offence since 1980) and the offence of making misleading statements were consolidated in the UK under the Criminal Justice Act 1993. On the pretext that this Act proved insufficiently flexible to deter and punish offenders properly, the FSMA 2000 created the additional civil offence of market abuse, requiring lower standards of proof than criminal offences. Both forms of offence relate to what might be described as 'misconduct' in the markets.

It can be argued that no firm should be allowed to permit its executives or others to trade using inside information because shareholders are not properly able to manage or control the activity as a result of the divorce between ownership and control in the modern company. There are a number of reasons why insider trading may be damaging. Insider trading may reduce economic efficiency (see, for example, Easterbrook, 1981) as insiders can gain from both bad news and good news in that they can deal on the basis of any news before the market generally becomes aware of it. As such, executives have an incentive to make a company's share price as volatile

however, and, as the chapter by Morrison in Booth (2009) and Norberg (2009) show, the activities of the rating agencies were seriously distorted by statutory regulation.

as possible, rather than to maximise the value of the company. It can also be argued that allowing insider trading provides an incentive for executives not to disseminate information.

A different form of argument in favour of rules preventing insider trading is essentially an 'equity' argument. Particular groups of shareholders, such as passive shareholders with small holdings, will suffer disproportionately if others are allowed to trade shares on the basis of inside information. Pritchard (2003) argues that insider trading can, in effect, be modelled as a transaction cost. There is no loss to 'outsiders' from insider trading unless an 'outsider' actually transacts. When he transacts, he takes a risk that the share is being bought from him at a lower price than is justified by fundamentals or being sold to him at a higher price than is justified by fundamentals (because there may be inside information that is not reflected in the price). If the share is not traded, there is no loss of value to the outsider because, in time, the inside information will become reflected in the price.

In theory, it should be possible to address insider-trading problems through voluntary contract. Firms themselves will raise their share price if they prohibit trading in their own shares by those who may have inside information – or perhaps they may prohibit all dealing in shares by executives. The enforcement of anti-insider-trading provisions through voluntary contract, however, may be problematic because of the costs of monitoring behaviour. Insider trading is very difficult to detect and firms that wish to prohibit it by contract will find it expensive to monitor contracts and perhaps to enforce contracts.

It should be noted, though, that any attempt to address the above problems through statutory action may impede the evolution of methods of corporate governance by restricting the contractual forms that exist within an organisation. These issues will be discussed further below. Also, as is discussed in Padilla (2002) and the references therein, it is not correct to argue that economies of scale in monitoring lead necessarily to the conclusion that insider trading should be subject to *statutory* regulation: exchanges could find their own solutions to this problem – if, indeed, it is regarded as a problem.

Hostile takeovers

There is one case in which shareholders may well be very happy to be kept in the dark about the purchase of shares by others, namely when the price of shareholders knowing that there is about to be a bid for a company is set against the price of their stewards (managers) knowing and thus being able to prepare anti-takeover action. Yet this is shareholders' precise predicament, courtesy of the FSA. Moves to acquire a company whose management has failed its shareholders are a matter for praise and not for criticism or the use of loaded words such as 'hostile'. Such actions should certainly not be discouraged by arbitrary legislation, such as levels of 'notification of interest', which play straight into the hands of the incumbent management. Whether existing regulations are right or wrong, it should be companies themselves (through their corporate governance mechanisms) and exchanges which develop those rules.

The Enron Corporation saga and other scandals

Under the criteria we have suggested above, some of the most infamous scandals would not rank as scandals at all, and their

Box 4 Is insider trading beneficial?

It seems to us that actions such as insider trading or market abuse are either fraudulent or not, and, if they are, they are covered by general law and contract law. There is nothing more peculiar about the financial services industry than there is about the vehicular services industry, where the seller may know more about a vehicle than the buyer (and methods of dealing with this problem, such as the provision of warranties, have evolved). Furthermore, even if we allow the industry a special status with a regulator that has the powers to develop its own codes and punishments, the definitions in those codes are very much of the Alice-in-Wonderland variety – 'it means what I say it means'. This substitutes 'The Rule of Men' for the Rule of Law.

The illogicality of criminalising insider *dealing* while not criminalising insider *non-dealing* (i.e. refraining from a deal that would have been made were it not for insider knowledge: something which it is impossible to prove or punish) is clear. Furthermore, the pursuit of diligent research is far less likely because of the fear of becoming contaminated as an insider and thus unable to deal.

Hence David Kynaston's classic 'white collar' (Kynaston, 2002: 776) crime is by no means the unqualified harm portrayed by the great and the good. Let us take two examples of insider dealing in a situation where a company prohibits directors from dealing in the company's shares:

(i) A company director learns that his company's operations have had a bad time recently and a profit warning is being prepared for delivery to the London Stock Exchange. The director sells shares in the company before the warning. This is a clear case of breach of contract in which information about the progress of the company itself was available to an *agent of the shareholders* who acted upon it prior to informing his principals.

(ii) Mr A is told by Mr B that Mr B (or Mr C) may bid for company X and buys the shares. There is no obligation for the possible bidder to actually bid or commit himself to a bid. The publication of all the musings (shared with friends or otherwise) of everybody considering any action, including making a bid for a company or not, is (thankfully for us all) an impossible task. Furthermore, the publication, or private notification, to the target's shareholders of such a possibility could result in action that could just as easily be regretted as celebrated. There is no point whatsoever in bringing this sort of action into criminal law and every point in letting shareholders select the rules of governance of not only their company but also the purchase and selling of its shares. In this environment we suggest that most shareholders will be concerned with the behaviour of their stewards rather than the changes in their share register.

These arguments suggest that the absence of private stock exchange and corporate governance arrangements to prevent insider dealing should not itself provide evidence for using state regulation.

perpetrators would have remained innocent. For example, take two of the most high-profile 'insider' scandals in the USA: those relating to Michael Milken and Martha Stewart.

In the mid-1980s Michael Milken used high-yield bonds to

back hostile takeovers in a perfectly reasonable and rational way but was defeated by an alliance of incumbent (and poor) managers, media hype and an SEC and government that were protecting established interests. After four years of pressure, he accepted a plea bargain on counts which *excluded* the original charges of insider trading and stock manipulation (Grant, 1999: 66–7).

Martha Stewart's circumstances were similar in that the original charges were dropped and she was convicted primarily of obstruction of justice – meaning that she lied to her tormentors when accused of insider trading even though she was entirely innocent of that charge. Might not you lie, out of entirely rational fear, in those circumstances? If you are stopped in the street and interrogated by armed policemen about shoplifting – of which you were entirely innocent – might you not say you were not in the vicinity even though you were?

The case against Kenneth Lay of Enron involved even more dubious tactics:

- Enron Corporation, formed in 1985 and soon to become one of the world's largest electricity and natural gas traders, filed for bankruptcy in December 2001.
- The underlying story is simple. Enron was originally a real energy company providing gas for Californian consumers. During the twenty years or so before it collapsed, Californian politicians made a huge mess of energy regulation, starting with requiring all utilities to take part of their power from highly expensive 'green' providers, thus forcing about $40 billion of wasted investment. The politicians also banned the construction of large power plants and in 1996 instructed all

utilities to *sell* their plants to independent merchants. They could then buy power from these merchants, but only in the spot market (no long-term contracts) via a single operator. Furthermore, prices to consumers had to be cut by 10 per cent and were then price-capped.

- Under a strangulation of language all this was called 'deregulation'. There was indeed *some* deregulation: utilities could trade power *among each other* and ship it across state lines at unregulated prices. These utilities soon split into grid companies (regulated) and generating companies (largely unregulated). The latter often and understandably moved out of California.
- Enron was adept at such manipulations but became increasingly speculative and came crashing down after the bull market ended.

Up to that point, however, Enron had enjoyed a long and mutually beneficial relationship with the US government for over a decade, including all the Clinton period. It is important to understand that part of the deal was exemption from crucial aspects of the Investment Companies Act, thus providing legal backing for its notorious off-balance-sheet budgeting. It also gained enormous tax-subsidised loans.

What has all this got to do with stock exchanges? Plenty, mainly in the shape of criticisms of the Securities and Exchange Commission (SEC), responsible for administering Federal Securities Laws in the USA:

- It seems inconceivable that the SEC didn't know about the legal privileges referred to above. Therefore one could expect it to keep an especially wary eye on Enron's accounting. But like all government regulators, the SEC had other fish to fry at the time.

- Stock exchanges competing on listing rules in a race to the top might well have banned much of the behaviour at Enron, in particular the accounting practices mentioned.
- Such stock exchanges would not have accepted favourable treatment in return for donations which at least must have fostered the view that Enron would not be allowed to go bankrupt and thus could take the wild risks it did.
- Such stock exchanges would not have turned love into hate overnight, as did the politicians to protect their backs and pursue dubious and populist targets.

On 25 May 2006 Kenneth Lay and Jeffrey Skilling, the two most senior former executives at Enron, were convicted for lying to investors. Lay subsequently died of a heart attack.

According to William Anderson,[7] 'the ultimate irony of the Lay–Skilling case is that they were convicted on criminal charges that were wrapped around legal activities'. Furthermore, the conviction of Lay for an 'illegal' stock sale is 'especially troubling' since his attorney advised him there was no need to report it. Indeed, Lay was still *buying* stock when advising employees to do the same; there is no evidence he was selling the stock or trying to jump ship. Anderson concludes that 'Lay and Skilling are hardly alone. The difference is that they are going to prison.'

Finally we mention two UK scandals which *were* scandalous. First, the Guinness–Distillers affair, in which Guinness directors

---

7   W. Anderson, 'Is Ken Lay really a criminal?', Mises Daily Article, 19 June 2006, www.mises.org.

promised privately that Guinness shareholders would stump up for any losses suffered by certain friends who supported the ramp in the Guinness share price with hard cash. This was clearly scandalous, but in essence it was a breach of contract with existing shareholders, whose agents they were. Under competitive private enterprise that contract would be entirely clear within the company and almost certainly would form part of the listing rules of any major stock exchange.

The consensus view of the establishment, including the press, on this scandal is well captured by Martin Waller in a Student Briefing in *The Times* of 4 November 2002: 'those who lost out were the buyers of the new [Guinness] shares who bought them in good faith, *valuing them with reference to the existing Guinness shares on the market*'. It is difficult to find sympathy with those adopting such a decision-making process.

The other colourful scandal which springs to mind is the Barings/Leeson affair which broke in February 1995, in which Nick Leeson's futures trading on the Singapore Stock Exchange racked up losses of several hundred millions of pounds and sank Barings. It can be argued that this was a one-off event of the type which will occur from time to time, and the Bank of England did well to resist forming a lifeboat. Kynaston's account, however, makes it perfectly clear that, to some extent, Leeson was carrying the can for his superiors. More importantly for us, an informal concession by the Bank of England had enabled Barings to 'use as much of its capital as it wished in sending margin payments to the Singapore Office' (Kynaston, 2002: 766). There was a major failure by the regulator.

Furthermore, J. K. Galbraith's 'bezzle' factor (Galbraith, 1955) is relevant. The degree to which stock market scandals arise late in booms (the correlation is very strong) means that those who cause the boom (central bankers) must take some of the blame. It is no exaggeration to say that booms distort financial and accounting data: the root of many scandals is boom-time activity which shows up as apparently genuine profit until the peak is close and the boom-time malinvestment is disclosed; businesses then become desperate and hope that they can ride out the worsened circumstances and return to what they have come to believe is normal. During the slow period of realisation that 'normal' is not what they thought it was, their behaviour becomes even more desperate, ending up with forms of deceit of which they would not have considered themselves capable in earlier times. The experience of the US stock market crash is instructive in this regard. It is now generally accepted that monetary laxity was the major cause of the 1920s stock market boom. The inevitable sharp correction and the following depression were made worse by US monetary policy being too tight. The stock market collapse was the spur to the creation of the SEC, yet the responsibility for the boom and bust can clearly be laid at the door of a government agency. There is a very real sense in which the creation of the SEC was a mistake – caused by a misunderstanding of the causes of the Great Depression.

These points demonstrate that the whole issue of insider trading and market abuse is highly subjective. Certain aspects of the problem involve fraud and can be dealt with under criminal and contract law if that is regarded as desirable. With regard to other aspects of insider trading and market abuse, different institutions may well wish to handle the issues differently, thus suggesting that non-statutory regulation and competition are the best way to deal with the problem. It is also very clear that the existence of extensive statutory regulation has far from eliminated scandals.

Is statutory regulation justified by conflicts of interest?

Both the EU and the FSA have examined 'conflicts of interest'.[8] One form highlighted is that which arises when an investment bank is giving buy/sell recommendations for a particular type of security and has a relationship with the company that has issued the securities. The question arises as to whether the broker has an incentive to provide 'biased' advice to help maintain good relationships with the company or, for example, to aid the process of underwriting a new securities issue with which the investment bank may be involved.

It is not clear why regulation here is necessary. Where conflicts of interest are inherent in the nature of a particular investment institution's business (for example, because they provide investment advice and also hold securities on their own book in a company on which they give advice), impartiality would have a market value. Lightfoot (2003) suggests that there is strong historical evidence that universal banks in the USA in the late 1920s were penalised because the securities they underwrote might be subject to conflicts of interest. If this is so, it is difficult to see why this should not apply more generally to conflicts of interest. A number of other studies provide evidence for this: see Crockett et al. (2003: 66) for a summary.[9] It is possible that monopoly

8   See FSA Discussion Paper no. 15, and earlier chapters.

9   The papers in that publication also suggest ways in which the market can overcome conflicts of interest, though the authors conclude that regulation to deal with conflicts of interest is appropriate in a range of financial markets. The authors also note that research-only investment houses, which do not have conflicts

power, concentrating investment research in a small number of diversified investment banks, may prevent such market mechanisms from working effectively (see Congdon, 2003). But if lack of competition is the problem, this should be tackled on its own terms: regulators should not deal with the symptoms by developing a special class of 'financial regulation'.

Institutional competition is probably the most effective way to deal with conflicts of interest. Some institutions might give totally independent advice (research boutiques). Others may not be independent but may have established and well-publicised mechanisms for dealing with conflicts of interest. Still others may have conflicts of interest but reveal them to clients. Finally, some institutions may choose to remain opaque and not to reveal conflicts of interest. Investment houses might also decide to employ people who have signed up to a particular professional code to which they can be held accountable. One would expect investors to take into account the potential for conflicts of interest when purchasing investment services. In so far as an institution seeks to mislead a client, this would be a matter for general law rather than for special financial regulation. Indeed, the FSA (2002: para. 4.8) recognises that such institutional competition exists, even in the current regulatory environment, so there is no obvious case for detailed statutory regulation.

Despite the observation of the FSA, it could be argued that institutional competition is inhibited by the existence of a statutory monopoly regulator. In so far as competition can take place in the current regulatory framework it does appear to do so. The

of interest, also produce more 'buy' recommendations, just as investment banks that have trading positions do (Crockett et al. 2003: 19), thus suggesting that this phenomenon may not simply be caused by conflicts of interest.

FSA acknowledges that many investment firms do choose to follow research analyst best-practice guidelines put out by bodies such as the Association of Investment Management and Research and the Securities Industry Association (ibid.: para. 7.3). Presumably this adds value to the services offered by investment firms. Furthermore (ibid.: para. 7.5), it is suggested that 'the market itself appears to be responding with a commercial operator announcing plans for regular publication of a "league table" of the accuracy of analysts' recommendations'. Nevertheless, the FSA has suggested, 'there is evidence that in certain cases analysts have compromised their integrity by issuing recommendations contrary to their own views' (ibid.: para. 3.9). Para. 4.10 of the FSA document also notes that researchers with institutions that also act as brokers or advisers to a company would give 80 per cent buy recommendations (compared with 45 per cent by brokers who are unconnected with their subject company). The absence of a perfect market, however, does not provide evidence that statutory regulation can improve market outcomes. After all, this FSA observation came after sixteen years of statutory regulation.

FSA (2002) refers to SEC regulations for the USA which were tightened up in 2002. Very detailed regulations relating to conflicts of interest were introduced affecting analyst compensation, providing restrictions on personal trading by analysts, and requiring disclosures by analysts of relationships with companies during television and radio interviews that refer to that company. Interestingly, the FSA notes that broker recommendations are more balanced in the UK – despite the greater degree of detailed regulation of the activities of investment institutions and their employees in the USA.

Conflicts of interest: regulators are not exempt!

Indeed, we should remember that statutory regulators have conflicts of interest too. For example, economic efficiency may demand a liberal approach but the self-interest of the regulatory bureau may lead the regulator to be over-cautious in regulating to avoid an event blowing up which may be blamed on the regulator.[10] Also, rather than pursue economic efficiency, regulatory bureaus have an incentive to increase their size. Participants in a market economy have an incentive to resolve conflicts of interest – even if the structure of a market leads to some conflicts persisting – whereas there are few effective incentives for regulatory bureaus to resolve their conflicts of interest.

Monopolies and cartels

If the prior assumption is that regulation of investment trans-actions and of those involved with transactions can take place through the activity of private exchanges, there might be concern that economies of scale and the necessity for exchanges to have a physical location might lead to a natural monopoly in the provision of stock exchange services. Also, because exchanges can limit access, in the same way that clubs can limit membership, they can act as cartels. Indeed, it has already been shown how it was competition and fair trading inquiries which led to the break-up of the pre-1986 system of private regulation in the UK and that, throughout the history of the London exchange, there

---

10 Of course, this conflict is exacerbated by the fact that the beneficial economic transactions that do not happen because of over-regulation are not noticed because they never take place, whereas problems that arise because of regulator inaction are obvious.

were complaints about limitations on access.

These arguments may have been valid at one time, but are much less valid today. Electronic trading significantly reduces costs and allows international competition (see Davis and Steil, 2001, for some discussion of this). Indeed, one of the drivers of the EU single market programme in this area is the desire to allow cross-border competition, although ironically the FSA (FSA, 2001: para. 3.9) argues that pan-EU competition requires a common approach to regulation.

Davis and Steil argue that the intensely competitive marketplace of electronic exchanges should ensure quality of the electronic systems underpinning the exchanges (losses as a result of systems failure could be huge because of the ability of investors to use other exchanges – as such, there are strong incentives for exchanges to regulate themselves). On the other hand, the FSA argues that it may have to put greater emphasis on the supervision of the management of IT systems because of potential losses to investors associated with failure: there is no evidence that this should be necessary.

Competition can also take place between recognised exchanges and non-exchange trading systems – the FSA suggests (ibid.) that this may require the introduction of comparable regulatory standards across exchange-based and non-exchanged-based trading systems. There seems to be no recognition that the existence of competition lessens the need for regulation.

It is certainly true that there are network effects and therefore advantages-of-scale economies in stock exchanges. It is increasingly true, however, that workable competition, if not perfect competition, is undermining the natural monopoly argument for regulating financial markets. The existence of electronic trading, non-exchange-based trading systems and international competition undermines monopoly power. The provision of exchange services is, in fact, a very competitive business and, as one of the functions of an exchange is to provide regulation, statutory regulation institutionalises monopoly power. But even if the arguments relating to natural monopoly were valid, the replacement of a private cartel or monopoly by a state monopoly regulator is not an unambiguous improvement.

If there are potential competition problems caused by a local exchange obtaining a significant share of securities business owing, perhaps, to economies of scale, these can be dealt with through the normal channels – preferably market-led, but otherwise the Office of Fair Trading, the Competition Commission and the courts. We should be wary, however, of breaking down traditional, evolved market structures because they give the appearance of giving rise to restrictive practices. Such structures are often an integral part of market-based regulation.

The functions of exchanges, clearing houses and so on are evolving over time. There is a growing tendency for the different parts of the system to specialise in particular functions (clearing, settlement and so on). There is also a tendency for more cross-border development of exchanges, clearing and settlement to reduce risk and reap economies of scale. This reduces the likelihood of monopoly but, in fact, global monopoly is not impossible – for example, in clearing and central counterparty functions. Nevertheless, these monopolies are contestable[11] and, in so far as they are involved in wholesale functions, they are used by well-capitalised, well-informed firms.

---

11 This point was made by David Hardy when group chief executive of LCH.Clearnet Ltd in a talk at the Sir John Cass Business School in 2004.

Different problems in mutual and proprietary exchanges

In a market where there is strong competition between different exchanges, there would, no doubt, be competition between governance systems of the exchanges too: both mutual and proprietary exchanges still exist, though the former are becoming much less common. In the real world, however, there may still be tensions between investors who use an exchange and its members or owners.

Regulations designed to ensure good governance of the exchange or, indeed, good corporate governance of companies whose securities are traded on an exchange may not help ensure equity between investors. These different objectives can conflict. Governments, in statutory law, sometimes put minority share-holder protection above corporate governance objectives in public policy (see, for example, Sternberg, 2004, for a discussion of this). For example, there is primary legislation that protects minority shareholder rights during a takeover. The compulsory notifica-tion of shareholdings above certain thresholds (for example, as required both in UK regulation and in the EU Transparency Directive) can also impair corporate governance while protecting minority shareholders. Anti-insider-dealing rules can also impair corporate governance but, on the other hand, ensure that all shareholders are on a level playing field. In the development of private regulation, proprietary exchanges would have to balance the net value that was added from regulations when they simulta-neously promote an objective such as investor protection – thus making the exchange more attractive to some investors – while impairing another objective, such as effective corporate govern-ance. Thus exchange-based regulation may not, for example, always protect the interests of small shareholders. If it is felt that special measures are necessary to protect the rights of small shareholders these should be dealt with by primary legislation, not by a financial regulator with unlimited powers. Such an issue is a public policy issue, in the same way that competition policy, 'disability rights' and so on are public policy issues. There seems to be no obvious case for a special monopoly statutory financial regulator to deal with these problems.

On balance, it is likely that a proprietary exchange would take less note of the interests of small investors and focus on developing rules that would maximise the value of a firm's shares when traded on an exchange. On the other hand, where exchanges are mutual bodies, Pritchard (2003) argues that the governance structure might encourage the exchange to be overprotective of small-scale investors. This arises because small-scale broker-dealers, working with retail investors, may have more votes in the exchange's governance system than larger-scale wholesale broker-dealers working with institutions, even though the value of the trades of the small-scale operators may be smaller. This would suggest that statutory moves to protect small-scale investors might not be necessary as long as there is competition between different forms of exchange.

The nature of exchanges has changed in the last two decades and it could be argued that the extent of 'off-exchange' trading and the separation of trading and clearing functions on exchanges have led to the concept of the self-regulating exchange becoming redundant. This is not so, however. One of the traditional purposes of exchanges is to develop the framework of rules by which their members or participants do business. That role has been taken over by statutory regulators and it is therefore hardly surprising that the nature and functions of exchanges have changed as their role in providing a regulatory framework has been taken away from them. As long as there are regulations that could be developed to the benefit of those trading in a class of investments, there are economic incentives for exchanges to develop to provide the regulatory framework in a competitive environment.

Problems of exchange-based rule-making

As in any organisation, there may be a temptation for members to bend or break the rules of an exchange if the expected costs from the penalties that can be imposed are less than the benefits from breaking the rules. The purpose of a system of market-based regulation is that the market mechanisms develop rules that, if they are followed by all participants, will be for the general good. It follows that, in many particular circumstances, an individual can gain, perhaps substantially, from breaking or bending particular regulations. It could be argued that the potential sanctions available to market-based regulators are insufficient to remove the incentives for rule-breaking. This could be for many reasons. The most likely reason is that particularly heavy sanctions used by a private regulator could be regarded as being in breach of general law or a restraint of trade. This should not, however, be an insurmountable obstacle. Sanctions used by other private regulatory bodies involve expulsion and very large fines – the most common examples are in the area of professional and amateur sport.

Is there an economic justification for any statutory regulation of exchange activity?

We have suggested above that most of the problems that arise from market-based regulatory systems can be addressed without recourse to a statutory regulator with specific responsibility for financial services. Competition issues can be dealt with by the competition authorities, regulations to protect specific classes of investor, if they are required, can be developed in basic law designed to address specific problems, and so on. Would there be anything left for a financial regulator? Oesterle (2000) suggests three possible functions. A financial regulator could enforce full disclosure of the mechanics of exchanges, their regulatory systems and the sanctions they use. It is arguable that a special financial regulator is not necessary for this purpose but, in any case, its reach would be limited in scope. Second, Oesterle suggests, the financial regulator should investigate and prosecute forms of fraud that have historically existed in trading markets. It is often the case that exchanges are appropriate mechanisms for developing particular rules of behaviour (for example, enforcing dealing at quoted prices) but are not appropriate mechanisms for preventing general forms of behaviour that undermine markets: that may be the purpose of the statutory authorities. In so far as this is true, where such behaviour involves fraud (for example, feeding misleading information to the market in order to gain from it) it should be dealt with by other statutory authorities under primary law rather than by a special financial regulator. Some form of prosecuting body that had specialist knowledge of and dealt only with financial services might, however, be appropriate. But this would take us beyond the scope of this monograph.

Finally, Oesterle suggests a role for a financial regulator in ensuring that markets are open and competitive. It is certainly not clear that this requires a specialist financial regulator. This is the domain of the Office of Fair Trading and the Competition Commission in the UK. Whether such a role for regulation of markets in general is desirable is debatable but also outside the scope of this monograph.

Has the FSA made its own case?

The FSA has not made a clear economic case for a state monopoly regulator of investment transactions. Llewellyn (1999) examines some general arguments for and against financial regulation but few of these are applied to the regulation of investment transactions.[12] This compares unfavourably with, for example, the Bank of England, which regularly produces rigorous, theoretical and practical economic justifications for different approaches to monetary policy management and for the use of independent central banks to achieve monetary policy objectives. Even the BBC publishes discussion on the economic issues relating to public service broadcasting, though their documents do not have the same air of authority or rigour as those of the Bank. The broadcasting and telecommunications regulator, Ofcom, regularly makes public statements about the limitations of regulators in correcting 'market failure' (see also its major study, Richards et al. (2006), which demonstrates an open-minded approach to many of these issues). If the FSA were to produce a rigorous justification for its role it would help it to develop its own framework of thinking and open up public debate.

---

12 FSA (2006), discussed below, was a welcome step forward in terms of its discussion of some aspects of the detailed case for regulatory intervention.

Clearly, as in any market, there is a role for the state in creating the legal framework. The enforcement of contracts, the prevention of fraud – which is, in effect, a form of theft – and so on are duties even of a minimal, liberal state. But while these functions may require specialist knowledge on the part of prosecutors, they do not require special financial regulators. As we have already made clear, the current approach of the FSA is an uneasy mix of regulatory powers, civil powers and powers to bring criminal prosecutions. So far we have found the arguments in favour of a statutory regulator unconvincing. There are further arguments against statutory regulation which tip the balance strongly.

9 THE CASE AGAINST GOVERNMENT REGULATION

Imperfect markets, perfect governments?

There are serious problems with government regulation. The 'market failure' approach to the analysis of securities regulation is pervasive in the FSA. Justifications for regulation are continually given in terms of perceived market failures. Indeed, the FSA could not be more explicit about this. Compare the following two statements:

> In meeting our objectives in a manner consistent with the principles of good regulation, we have adopted a regulatory approach based on correcting market failure ... There are, however, numerous cases where unregulated financial markets will not achieve the best outcome due to some form of market failure, making action on our part necessary.
> (FSA, 2003)

> One reason often given to justify Government intervention is that a particular market could be improved because it is 'failing'. The implication is that the Government should step in to improve on the free working of the market. But the perfect market does not exist and there are many reasons why Government intervention can make the situation worse ... Regulatory failure can be worse than market failure. Both need to be considered carefully before any intervention.
> (Better Regulation Task Force, 2003)

Both quotes are from reports of different government bodies published in the same month.

It is worth noting that the then chairman of the FSA, Callum McCarthy, said in a speech in 2004 (see FSA, 2005a: 12) that the market failure analysis that the FSA had previously enunciated was a weak justification for intervention. He then went on to make a point not very different from the point made by the Better Regulation Task Force. The FSA has since produced a document on market failure (see FSA, 2006) in which the analysis sits somewhere between the philosophies implied by the two quotes above but which certainly uses what it describes as 'market failure analysis' in coming to a view on regulation.

Like the idea of perfect competition, the market failure approach is vacuous – literally empty of meaning.[1] In the absence of a so-called 'perfect market', it cannot be known what the outcome of such a market would have been because there are undiscovered opportunities for increasing welfare. The dispersed knowledge of markets cannot be centralised within government agencies, and if there are undiscovered opportunities for increasing welfare, government cannot know what they would have been.

Therefore, government action cannot correct for market failure because it does not know the objective that it is seeking to achieve: it does not and cannot know what the outcome of a perfectly competitive market, without 'market failure', would have been. Furthermore, no market can or does adhere to the idealised textbook model of perfect competition; thus the regulator can

---

1 See, for example, the discussion in the Better Regulation Task Force report (2003), and, of course, the Austrian literature on the meaning of competition, such as that by Kirzner and Hayek.

use the market failure doctrine as an excuse for controlling every aspect of a market process. In addition, those acting on behalf of government will themselves have objectives that they wish to pursue. They will not necessarily act in the best interests of those participating in the market, even if they know what their best interests are. It is of particular concern that the FSA regarded market failure as making action by the regulator *necessary* when they could have used a phrase such as 'creates an a priori case for investigating whether regulation would be appropriate', 'or may provide some justification for considering regulation'.

Some of these issues are identified by the public choice economics literature (see, for example, Tullock et al., 2000). It is widely assumed that governments need to regulate to address certain so-called 'imperfections' in markets. Those 'imperfections' arise, in large part, because individuals indulge in 'maximising behaviour' in a context where such behaviour gives rise to social costs and benefits, exploitation of monopolistic positions, etc. Liberal markets, it is argued, in certain circumstances, provide incentives for behaviour that is not optimal from an economic welfare point of view, and thus government must intervene.

In the mainstream literature, however, remarkably little attention is given to whether regulators face incentives to produce sub-optimal outcomes and whether they make an imperfect situation worse. Public choice economics recognises that we do not have a choice between imperfect markets and the same markets as perfected by regulators but a choice between two imperfect institutional settings: imperfect markets operating under the rule of general law, and regulated markets, regulated by self-interested people controlled by a very imperfect process of democracy. Regulators are rational maximisers with imperfect knowledge. The behaviour of maximising groups in the regulatory framework (whether regulators themselves, politicians or large firms that try to capture the regulator) and the absence of perfect knowledge among regulators mean that the concept of the imperfect regulator handsomely complements that of the imperfect market.

Maximising regulators do not have appropriate incentives to provide the optimal amount and type of regulation. For example, regulators may be risk-averse because promotion within the regulatory authority may arise if a group of regulators have avoided the failure of financial institutions. In terms of the prudential regulation of financial institutions, this may manifest itself in incentives to limit financial failures below the level that consumers would prefer. In terms of the regulation of financial markets, it may manifest itself by an inclination to over-regulate to avoid scandal and market abuse. In either case the problem is likely to manifest itself in over-regulation – the provision of detailed rule-making which imposes direct regulatory costs, as well as costs of compliance, on users of financial markets and which constrains innovation.

The optimal number of failures of financial institutions or the optimal number of scandals may be lower for government officials than for market participants. The costs of additional regulation are diffuse and will rarely generate strong objections from market participants. Additional regulation may reduce the probability of failure, however, and thus increase the chance of advancement for officials. Furthermore, statutory regulators can come under the influence of well-organised interest groups that may exert undue pressure. In particular, market incumbents may favour more regulation if that regulation raises the cost to new entrants to the market.

Given that the absence of a perfect market is complemented by the absence of omniscient, beneficent regulators who can perfect the market, it is important that the right framework exists to enable the process of competition to discover the optimal regulatory structures. Private financial regulation can evolve as part of a competitive process that is absent with state regulation.

The FSA has at least considered these issues now (see FSA, 2006). The FSA quotes Arthur and Booth (2006), which develops the arguments summarised above. It rejects the arguments saying,

> The criticism that the government or regulator cannot know the outcome of the perfectly efficient market and cannot sensibly use MFA [Market Failure Analysis] to pursue it seems irrelevant because the FSA is not trying to create perfect markets (which may never exist) or their outcomes; the FSA is using MFA for the more modest goal of pursuing its statutory objectives in a way that is likely to lead to welfare improvements. (FSA, 2006: 45)

In principle, this may seem like a reasonable argument. It is not necessary to know where the end point of 'perfect competition' would lead to be able to assess the value of an incremental move in the right direction. It may be possible to identify ways in which markets fail, examine the structural causes of the failure and regulate to improve the outcome. There are, however, at least three flaws in the FSA's approach to this.

A cost–benefit analysis is the method by which a judgement whether or not to intervene would be made by the FSA. While it is welcome that an economic framework for analysis is being employed, such a framework cannot do the job of determining whether a market intervention will increase welfare. If a regulation prevents a market solution developing we cannot know the welfare cost of preventing the development of market institutions. Interestingly, the FSA recognises this point, proposing that its employees become familiar with Coase (1960, 1974) – but this does not resolve the problem. Also, if an intervention inhibits competition[2] in any way, we cannot know the welfare cost caused by the reduction in competition. This is precisely for the reason stated in Arthur and Booth (2006): market competition will lead to the creation of welfare-enhancing developments that are unknown before they originate.

Finally, when judging whether to make an intervention, the FSA recognises that the costs of regulation might outweigh the benefits. Indeed, this is its definition of regulatory failure. Of course, if we cannot assess the costs and benefits of regulation, we cannot determine whether there is regulatory failure, so defined. Regulatory or government failure, however, is a wider institutional concept. The FSA believes that markets fail and thus need to be corrected by regulation – because, it argues, in some circumstances they cannot correct themselves. Regulatory failure is institutional and thus cannot be corrected by any body. It arises from imperfect knowledge by the regulator, agency problems and information asymmetries. The regulator cannot know all the costs and benefits of regulatory action because imperfect information afflicts regulators to an even greater extent than it afflicts markets – because information that is dispersed in the market cannot be centralised within a regulator. Regulators are very imperfectly accountable to those whom they are intended to serve. Also, regulators have far more information than those to whom they are accountable (the government) and those whom they are expected

---

2   For example, by raising the cost of entry.

to serve (investors) about the costs and benefits of their activities, so information asymmetries between regulatory institutions and those they are trying to serve are embedded within the system and cannot be overcome. No amount of market failure analysis and cost–benefit analysis can correct this institutional failing.

The most effective way to overcome so-called market failures is through the process of competition, including the *potential* for competition that always exists unless it is prohibited. We argue that it is only through regulatory competition that the problems of 'regulator failure' can be overcome. Furthermore, investment market regulation is particularly amenable to regulatory competition.

Regulatory competition

We do not know the best structures for delivering regulation or the best regulatory framework and sets of detailed rules, *ex ante*. We can make some educated guesses and we can use economic theory[3] as a guide but we do not know in advance what the best structures, frameworks and rules are. We currently have a state monopoly provider of regulation – the FSA. Top-down, state-created structures cannot determine the optimal regulatory structure. This may seem like a glib point – an attempt to use terms such as 'optimal' and 'competition' developed by economists for analysing decisions such as those relating to the number and type of bananas consumers may wish to buy in the wrong context. It is not. There are some issues relating to regulation that naturally

---

3   Centrally planned, communist economies can use economic theory as a guide to the central planning board when setting prices but it does not lead to efficient resource allocation.

belong with the criminal and civil law and the statutory authorities. For the most part, however, financial regulation involves the provision of a set of services in the same way that railway through ticketing and the timetable are sets of regulatory services in a different context. The notion of competition is highly relevant.

Arguments are often put forward to suggest that regulatory competition leads to a 'race to the bottom'. There is no evidence for this. Indeed, former chairman and CEO of the FSA Howard Davies said (Davies, 2002):

> The argument that we hear is that regulatory competition cannot be allowed in the EU. Why not? Because, I am told, we would see regulatory arbitrage and a 'race to the bottom'. That seems highly unlikely to me, especially at a time when investors are, not unreasonably, nervous about unconventional corporate structures and opaque accounts. Furthermore, our regime, tougher in these respects than others in the EU, has attracted mobile capital, far from repelling it.

These arguments surely apply at the level of private regulators, such as exchanges, if they apply to competition between state regulators. Surely they also apply to issues such as accounting (see Myddelton, 2004), disclosure and corporate governance (see Sternberg, 2004).

Competition between firms for capital should lead to the evolution of appropriate standards rather than an erosion of all standards. Indeed, evidence that different investors value different forms of regulation rather than necessarily wanting tighter or looser regulation comes from a report published by the City of London (London Stock Exchange/Oxera, 2006). Oxera found that small and early-stage companies preferred more liberally regulated environments (as they have no track record and satisfying additional regulations would be expensive). On the other hand, for other companies, a more stringent listing regime may have offsetting advantages (signalling quality and investor confidence), resulting in a lower cost of capital. These issues are considered further below.

One obvious case against a single statutory regulatory body is that it prevents competition in rule development. Such regulatory competition is often described, in rather derogatory terms, as 'regulatory arbitrage'. Where regulation is developed to protect those who are not party to regulated investment transactions, regulatory arbitrage may happen. There is no reason to believe that it will happen where such externalities are generally limited in their effects to holders and transactors of securities.

Indeed, competition is *required* to discover the best form of regulation. Different methods of regulation impose different costs on market users and constrain innovation to differing degrees. The objectives of regulation can be achieved by direct regulation, supervision or monitoring. Direct regulation can involve rules to restrain or require certain forms of behaviour or the creation of incentives for firms to behave in a particular way (Llewellyn, 1999). It is by no means clear which approach is appropriate for achieving the different objectives of regulation, and a competitive process is surely the best way of discovering the best approach.

If financial regulation, whether private or statutory, is primarily developed to deal with externalities – where the behaviour of one transactor impacts on others in the market – it can be argued that rules systems developed by the market institutions themselves can internalise such externalities whereas statutory regulation frequently imposes externalities on others. We cannot be sure of discovering the best rule system easily, and competition between different rules systems can help facilitate the development of the best systems.

For many years, the London Stock Exchange had an effective monopoly of investment trading business. As a result, *inter alia*, of deregulation of capital flows, freer trade in services and changes in technology, however, there is greater competition across exchanges. Such competition could facilitate the development of an optimal regulatory framework for those dealing in investments. Competing exchanges exist in the form of NASDAQ, pan-European exchanges, AIM and the London Stock Exchange main market. All these are in competition with off-exchange trading. Because companies can choose where to list, there is also competition between different geographical regulatory jurisdictions, although such competition is being undermined by the emphasis on harmonisation within the EU.

The benefits of exchanges providing systems of rules are discussed in Pritchard (2003). Exchanges can help create trust that leads to deep and liquid securities markets by designing transparent trading mechanisms, monitoring trading, imposing disclosure standards on quoted companies and enforcing rules. These features, as well as integrity and reputation, are important marketing tools for an exchange. Such functions do not have to be performed by a statutory monopoly regulator. La Porta et al. (2006) provide an interesting comparison of state and private regulatory enforcement mechanisms for securities markets. They conclude that state laws requiring disclosure, etc., are important but that private enforcement, so that investors obtain restitution for damages and losses incurred through enforcement of private contracts, fosters more robust markets.

Scandals, unintended consequences and trust
State regulations and scandals

State regulation and scandals are inextricably intertwined, each feeding off the other. State regulation in any area starts off lightly and tightens in response to scandals, thus adding another turn of the screw. Each turn of the screw is a 'one-off', a few years at best after the previous one, whereas the market is a continuing process of discovery and adjustment. Scandals can increase as state regulations tighten because the regulation is often misdirected and crowds out other natural mechanisms – not the least of which is trust (see below). There may be a lack of trust and virtue within markets at any one particular time. But if this is so, statutory regulation is simply not an instrument that is designed to deal with this problem. This view was articulated effectively, as it happens, in the Catholic Bishops of England and Wales general election document: 'In place of virtue we have seen an expansion of regulation. A society that is held together just by compliance to rules is inherently fragile, open to further abuses which will be met by a further expansion of regulation' (Bishops' Conference of England and Wales, 2010: 7).

Furthermore, state regulation corrupts enterprise (as public choice theory predicts) and forces innocent people to attempt to circumvent rules that favour their competitors. Moreover, state regulation is often adopted without cost–benefit analysis and, when state regulators do undertake cost–benefit analysis or regulatory impact assessments, they can never quantify costs and benefits effectively. State regulation creates barriers to entry and hits small business hardest. And it creates an atmosphere of fear.

Nowhere is this more true than in business and finance. Coupled with *unlimited* democracy, state regulation can

Box 5 **Even the regulators believe in (limited) regulatory competition**

It is not only the former chairman and chief executive of the FSA, Howard Davies, who believes in the power of regulatory competition (see above). Recently, there have been a number of discussions about the regulation of AIM. It is clear from these discussions that the role of AIM as a regulating exchange is taken very seriously. The LSE understands that AIM will lose business if it is seen to be either too lightly or too heavily regulated. In 2006, the rules for obtaining a quotation on AIM were changed in the following way:

- A rule book was published outlining the Nominated Advisers' precise responsibilities.
- Nominated Advisers' duties are required to be published on the front of an admission document for an AIM-quoted company.
- The LSE doubled the amount it can fine Nominated Advisers and introduced a formal disciplinary letter.
- Nominated Advisers have to keep a company website.
- AIM-quoted companies have to create a website within six months.

In early 2007, Roel Campos, a commissioner on the US Securities and Exchange Commission, strongly criticised AIM.[1] He described the market as a casino and then said, 'It is a losing proposition to tout lower standards as a way to promote your markets' (*The Times*, 9 March 2007). This statement seems odd. He is criticising a competing market which, according to his own reasoning, will gain business from the markets he

---

1   It should be noted that the criticisms were rebutted.

regulates, if it takes heed of the criticism! Interestingly, Campos also made a strong case for the role of 'reputation' as a force to spur effective regulatory competition (see also below) as he suggested that the main London Stock Exchange might suffer if AIM was seen to be too lightly regulated because of the perceived joint branding. Why does Campos need to comment on this matter? If he is right, his markets will gain business from the failure of AIM and the London Stock Exchange. But also, if he is right, then it shows that regulatory competition is effective and there is therefore no need for statutory regulators.

criminalise decent citizens (such as Michael Milken and Martha Stewart) and makes them walk the plank in public.

Thus David Kynaston, even though he does not appear to fully appreciate the differences between regulation by the state, 'self-regulatory organisations' and the market, remarks: 'More than a quarter of a century after the secondary banking crisis it was still a moot point whether all the ensuing regulatory legislation and heartache had rendered the City a fundamentally cleaner place – not least in the ever-vexed area of frequently perpetrated, infrequently prosecuted insider dealing, still the classic white-collar crime' (Kynaston, 2002: 776).

The 'law of unintended consequences'

The 'law of unintended consequences' featured prominently on the website of the UK Cabinet Office's former Regulatory Impact Unit. The phrase related to the unintended consequences of state regulation. It was acknowledged that consequences may or may not be predictable, and there was a section on 'Alternatives to regulation'. Listed 'alternatives' included price caps, taxes, subsidies and rewarding desirable behaviour! They also included *compulsory* information provision, education (or labelling), 'self-regulation' (see above), co-regulation, quasi-regulation and regulatory reform orders; in other words the 'alternatives' are largely alternative *types* of state regulation, not alternatives *to* state regulation. The Regulatory Impact Unit and its predecessor, the Better Regulation Task Force, are to be congratulated, however, for being honest about the failings of direct state regulation.[4]

Unintended consequences of state regulation arise because regulators face the same problems as central planners in socialist societies – they cannot predict with a reasonable degree of certainty the results of their actions because all the knowledge necessary to make such predictions is naturally dispersed and cannot be centralised. It is therefore helpful to have adaptive systems of regulation and systems of regulation where the interests of the regulator are reasonably well aligned with the interests of those in whose interest the regulator is supposed to be acting. We argue that private exchanges can provide such a system more effectively than statutory regulation.

Northern Rock and unintended consequences

A good example of the unintended consequences of regulation occurred in the recent Northern Rock run – and another example is given in Box 6. It is not unreasonable that the owners of banking businesses, and their customers, might regard it as being in their

---

4   In earlier publications it had proposed the alternative of not regulating at all.

mutual best interests not to be informed when events were taking place that might imply that the business is in difficulty. Of course, *ex post*, it will always have been in the best interests of those shareholders or customers who can act most quickly to have been told. If the actions of the few who can act quickly endanger the value of the business for remaining owners and customers, however, then the consensus, *ex ante*, might be that it is better for the business to deal with its problems without them being made public – at least for a time. This approach may maximise the probability that, when particular events that have an adverse impact on the business happen, value in the business is preserved. Exchanges could therefore develop their own rules, which may be different for banks than for other businesses, regarding the type of price-sensitive information that should be disclosed and when it should be disclosed.[5]

In the case of Northern Rock, as the governor of the Bank of England, Mervyn King, told the House of Commons Treasury Select Committee on 19 September 2007, the Bank of England believed it was prevented from acting covertly as a lender of last resort by the EU Market Abuse Directive (indeed, it is likely that, if that Directive had not existed, FSA rules would have prevented the Bank from acting covertly in any case). At best the situation was extremely unclear when it needed to be crystal-clear. When the Bank of England announced that it was providing lender-of-last-resort facilities, as it believed it had to, the run on Northern

---

5   In the same way that all the passengers on a tube train might agree that when a passenger was found to be carrying a bomb, this fact is not announced explicitly by those conducting an evacuation. Though the lucky ones might get away first, the disorderly evacuation that such knowledge might cause might raise the probability that the evacuation is considerably slower than it would otherwise have been.

Rock and a series of further, very serious problems ensued. Mervyn King also believed he was hindered in proposing various actions to resolve the Northern Rock case by the Takeover Code, which became statutory in 2006 as a result of EU initiative.[6]

This is not an argument in favour of central banking or the provision of lender-of-last-resort facilities. It is an argument in favour of companies being allowed to develop their own systems of corporate governance, in the context of the rules that exchanges develop, which are appropriate to the nature of the company.

The economic point here is that regulations relating to the trading of shares, the announcement of price-sensitive information, etc., do carry externalities. Some people may suffer or gain if there are parties who receive that information before others. Those externalities, however, are more or less confined to shareholders themselves. It is therefore possible for a company (in its Articles of Association or elsewhere) or an exchange to determine the best set of rules that maximise the value for all shareholders. In the case of Northern Rock, specific and detailed statutory regulations impeded the provider of lender-of-last-resort facilities. There is no reason why banks should not have different rules from (say) sausage-making companies in respect of what information should be released to shareholders and how, and these rules do not need to be determined by statutory regulators.

Transparency, accountability and trust

In the 2002 Reith Lectures, Professor Onora O'Neill argued that the 'twin gods of transparency and accountability' were

---

6   See Congdon (2008) for a discussion of the EU role in this affair more generally.

undermining the far more potent quality of trust. This is indeed a crucial point. It is not as if all three can be used without detriment to each other (see also Daykin, 2004, who articulated a comprehensive case for trust, rather than regulation, in the financial sector). Trust, if justified, represents an incredibly powerful short cut to voluntary exchange and trade. Trust is the real thing: transparency and accountability are at best pale shadows involving a lot of hard work to provide information to platoons of busybodies as well as those with a genuine financial interest. In practice accountability and transparency are far less effective than trust; for the untrustworthy it means a relatively small amount of work to devise a few smokescreens.

As Daniel Klein points out (Klein, 2000), a 'Truster' doesn't care about asymmetry of information: he or she merely needs 'pointed information' – such as where to find a trustworthy financial adviser. Klein also points out that problems of trust can be resolved in a number of powerful ways, including middlemen (like the best retailers), extended dealings, brands, a reputational nexus (it doesn't take too long to find somebody who knows somebody else who ...), specialist information providers such as *Which?* or investment monitors, seals of approval (Kitemarks), and so on. Other trust problems can be eliminated or reduced by repackaging the product – providing free trials or test drives, warranties, samples, sponsored chat-groups, and so on. 'The Small Deal Stock Exchange is a big deal: an exchange you can trust' might be a slogan we could expect to see if there were competition between exchanges and the elimination of statutory regulation.

Box 6 Unintended consequences – government regulation of pensions

If we want to examine the unintended consequences of regulations, we need look no farther than the havoc wreaked by the government regulation of pensions.

The story starts with the Maxwell scandal and the government response through the 1995 Pensions Act. This brought in the Minimum Funding Requirement, which itself had unintended consequences. The Act also required trustees to ensure that pensions payable to retired members were paid in full before any obligations were fulfilled to members who were not in receipt of their pensions. This and earlier legislation also increased the 'quality' of pension-fund promises to their members – for example, by requiring limited price indexation of pensions.

We see the impact of this today as thousands of workers have lost all their pension entitlements. Consider the following example. A pension fund has 75 per cent of liabilities due to existing pensioners (for example, an old industrial company with an ageing workforce) and 25 per cent of liabilities due to active members. The fund has a 20 per cent deficit. If the company winds up, the entire deficit is borne by the active members. The pensioners receive 100 per cent of their benefits, active members will lose 80 per cent of their benefits – creating an enormous discrepancy between members whose retirement dates may be only a day or two apart!

Subsequently, the government has increased costs of pension funding still further by a number of measures intended to 'help' members. Benefits have been made still more 'secure' through a Pension Protection Fund, financed by a levy on sound schemes and by the calculation of deficits on a strict funding standard. It is now virtually impossible for a company to deal with deficits by reducing the real value of members' benefits slightly.

As a result of these aspects of regulation, risks to active members of pension schemes have become *much* greater. Furthermore, most of the schemes have been closed down by their sponsoring companies. Defined benefit schemes provided the best and most secure benefits relative to salary – albeit with a limited amount of risk-sharing. The attempt by government to regulate away this risk-sharing aspect of the schemes has led to employees being moved to vastly inferior and riskier schemes. The irony, of course, is that the spark that led to this legislation was a *fraud* by Robert Maxwell. This was already illegal and none of the regulations that have had such an adverse effect had anything to do with the cause of the losses in the Maxwell scandal. To quote from Byrne et al. (2006: 9): 'There is no point in having the best regulation in the world if there are no schemes left to regulate.'

Costs of regulation

It is not feasible to produce an estimate of the costs and benefits of statutory financial regulation. If there were no statutory regulation then clearly the costs of the statutory system would not be incurred. There are, however, five aspects to the counterfactual that it is not possible to cost. The first is the cost of market innovation that does not take place because of the presence of regulation. Second, this monograph does not advocate an absence of regulation but proposes that the market is capable of generating its own regulation – this would, of course, have a cost. Third, there are the costs of inhibiting competition between regulatory systems, which could lead to better regulation and innovation in regulatory approaches. Fourth, there are the costs arising from the failure of investment firms to focus on consumer needs as a result of regulatory requirements being the driving force of business practice.[7] Finally, there are costs of regulation that are imposed on investment firms and consumers that are very difficult to quantify. It is worth, however, noting the direct cost of running the FSA. The total budgeted cost of the FSA for 2009/10 is £413.8 million. Of this figure approximately one third could perhaps be attributed to the regulation of wholesale investment markets, though the organisational structure is now so complex it is very difficult to tell. What is alarming, though, is the increase in cost of the FSA (see Table 1).

In recent years in particular, despite low levels of inflation, there have been considerable increases in costs and staff. Overall, in the six years to the end of 2010/11, total costs will increase by 115 per cent and total staff by 51 per cent. A big proportion of this increase is a consequence of the increased role that the regulator has sought as a result of its perceived failures at the time of the financial crash. It is also notable that the increase in budget is much greater than the increase in staff numbers (even after adjusting the budget for inflation).

---

7   To give one anecdotal example, it took one of the authors seven weeks to have a small cheque paid into a personal pension scheme as a result of checks undertaken to satisfy money-laundering regulations. Any checks were clearly unnecessary – the cheque was small, paid out of a bank account that had been open for twenty years, it was paid into a pension scheme the proceeds of which could not be used for another thirteen years, and the scheme was attached to an employer scheme already receiving contributions. The focus of the company, however, was clearly on satisfying any small risk of falling foul of regulatory rules – retrospectively applied – rather than providing a service to the customer.

Table 1 **The growth of the FSA**

Year	Total budget (£m)	Growth on previous year (%)	Total staff	Growth on previous year (%)
2001/02	195.8		2,030	
2002/03	194.0	–1	2,095	3
2003/04	215.4	11	2,200	5
2004/05	211.0	–2	2,165	–1
2005/06	266.0	26	2,425	12
2006/07	274.1	3	2,600	7
2007/08	300.1	9	2,700	4
2008/09	320.7	7	2,740	1
2009/10	413.8	29	2,800	2
2010/11	454.7	10	3,260	16

'Regulatory Impact Assessments'

The FSA undertakes Regulatory Impact Assessments (RIAs) of the costs and benefits of regulation. These are conceptually flawed. The direct costs of regulation may be quantifiable – though the fact that it is the regulator itself which commissions the RIA, and that the costs of regulation are highly subjective, should be of concern. The costs of regulation, however, in terms of the impact on competition and innovation of imposing uniform practices, are not calculable. The counterfactual of what would happen if there were no regulation cannot be defined because we cannot know what innovations would have developed in the absence of regulation. The benefits of regulation are also extremely subjective.

The RIA presented to the Economic Secretary to the Treasury relating to the EU Prospectus Directive 2005 is instructive.

Incremental one-off costs of £2.3 million and ongoing costs of £7.55 million per annum are identified – essentially paperwork costs. The benefits are described as 'unquantifiable', with reference being made to a 0.5 per cent reduction in the cost of capital from the full implementation of the directive. No mention was made of the unquantifiable costs of inhibiting innovation and competition in information provision. If the RIA had mentioned this as a cost, it would have looked comical. On the cost side, there would have been huge 'unquantifiable costs' plus estimated costs of £7.55 million. On the benefits side there would have been huge 'unquantifiable benefits' plus a benefit of a 0.5 per cent reduction in cost of capital if the single market, of which the Prospectus Directive is a small part, is implemented. One must call into question the RIA as an analytical tool.

The EU did no assessment of the costs and benefits of the Markets in Financial Instruments Directive (MiFID). One estimate has put the cost of MifID at £6.5 billion by 2010 – the estimates in the study in which this was quoted, however, varied from £1.2 billion to £65 billion (see Boyfield, 2006). RIAs are clearly not reliable given the huge range of cost and benefit estimates that can be produced. The discipline of developing an RIA may be useful given our existing regulatory framework, but the fact that such tools have to be relied upon undermines the argument for maintaining that framework.

A study of the cost of regulation was published by the FSA (Europe Economics, 2003). It produced interesting output but does not help us in our analysis of whether state regulation is better than market regulation for the reasons discussed above. Europe Economics found that, for the median firm, compliance costs for all regulated firms were about 1.6 per cent of their total costs.[8, 9] Only a small minority of firms regarded FSA regulation as important in determining service quality. Rather worryingly, the median level of regulatory costs for small firms was three times that for large firms. This suggests that regulation could encourage acquisitions and discourage new entry and competition. Though regulatory costs are a relatively small proportion of total costs, they are, of course, a high proportion of profit margin, indicating that the impact on competition could be important: for small firms, regulatory costs of this level could be 50 per cent of a typical profit margin. Most firms identified brand and service quality as the main factors that gave them a competitive advantage, suggesting that regulation is not necessary to make most firms behave appropriately.[10]

We will not discuss the issue of costs of different regulatory systems further, as it is not possible to compare regulatory systems simply on the basis of cost and it is not intended to do so. Different regulatory systems provide different bundles of services at different costs. Merely comparing the costs without comparing the value of the packages of regulatory services would be a futile exercise. Nevertheless, it is clear that statutory regulation imposes significant costs on businesses – especially small businesses – and that those costs are not effectively controlled in a 'public choice' environment.

---

8   Total costs are, in fact, total costs excluding regulatory costs.

9   This is the figure for all regulated firms. Firms conducting investment business were close to the median for all firms.

10 The most comprehensive work on regulation is probably that related to the tax system, which suggests that regulation costs for small businesses are sixteen times the cost to the largest businesses as a proportion of turnover: see Chittenden et al. (2010).

Conclusion

There are convincing arguments in favour of private regulation of investment transactions and persuasive arguments against state regulation. There are clearly areas where private markets will not provide the 'optimal' level of regulation – but all markets fall short of the theoretical ideal of 'perfect competition': as such its value as a theoretical paradigm in this context is questionable. Governments fail too. They can institutionalise the failings of markets yet do not have the information or ability to behave in a disinterested fashion to effectively correct so-called market failure. Furthermore, governments impede the very processes that allow markets to discover solutions that increase welfare. Government regulation frequently has unintended consequences and impedes the development of virtues that markets encourage, such as the virtue of trust.

10 CONCLUSION

The crash and the future of financial regulation

Before concluding, it is worth asking whether recent events in financial markets strengthen the case for a statutory financial regulator with wide-ranging powers. It is difficult to believe that they do. As has been noted above, FSA investment market regulations applied to all listed companies. This was so even if those regulations were not appropriate, as might well have been the case for banks. The FSA tripped up the Bank of England when the latter tried to alleviate the problems at Northern Rock. Also, if anything, the crisis has strengthened the case for returning the regulation of banks to that institution – the Bank of England – that provides lender-of-last-resort facilities.[1] The FSA would then lose a major function and the rationale for a single financial regulator would be undermined.

The crisis has also provided some evidence that institutions with wide-ranging regulatory functions and objectives fall prey to the public choice problems that we have described. Additionally, it can be argued that regulators with wide-ranging powers do not focus sufficiently on the narrow range of problems that can provide an a priori justification for statutory financial market regulation. With this in mind it is interesting to note how

---

1   Assuming that the central banking model is going to remain.

unfocused the FSA's response to the financial market crash has been. Its response has included proposals for a significant expansion of regulation of the sale of UK mortgages despite the fact that there is no evidence that UK mortgage debts had anything to do with the crisis.[2] Only one third of a page of the 126-page Turner Review (Turner, 2009) related to the key issue of ensuring the orderly failure of insolvent banks – much of the rest of the policy-related chapters of the Turner Review related to peripheral issues.

Finally, the regulation of investment markets was not really associated with the crash. Overall, nothing that has happened since 2007/08 does anything other than strengthen the argument in this monograph.

Regulation by accident

We conclude that there is no strong justification for a statutory regulator of securities and investment markets. There is a need for regulation and there is a need for certain principles of criminal law, contract law, common law and civil law to be applied. Indeed, two interesting conclusions of a recent detailed report (City of London, 2009) are that common-law legal systems are better than civil-law systems for protecting minority shareholder rights and that robust systems of financial regulation increase return on equity. Arguably, in the long run, wide-ranging statutory regulation undermines the common law and thus undermines shareholder rights. Private regulation, on the other hand, is not incompatible with either robust regulation or a continuation of common-law traditions.

---

2   See: http://www.fsa.gov.uk/pubs/discussion/fs10_01.pdf and http://www.fsa. gov.uk/pubs/discussion/dp09_03.pdf.

A convincing case for a single statutory financial regulatory authority with oversight of securities and investment markets has not been found. Furthermore, it is certainly not clear that the principles by which the FSA operates are designed to achieve appropriate economic objectives of regulation in the field of securities transactions. This is perhaps not surprising. The FSA was never created in its current form as a result of an analysis of the economic merits of private and statutory regulation in this area. The original self-regulatory organisations were set up because of dissatisfaction with the order of things that existed at that time. The FSA was then set up because of dissatisfaction with the performance of the so-called self-regulatory organisations. It was dissatisfaction with their role in banking, financial products sales and insurance regulation, however, and the perceived need for a unified regulator to deal with these areas, which created the momentum for a single financial regulator. It is difficult to point to any evidence from the UK or the USA that justifies a single, statutory regulator of securities markets. There is a similar haphazard history in the USA. The statutory regulatory framework was set up as a result of a mistaken understanding of the causes of the Great Depression.

It is perhaps for this reason that confusion seems to reign in terms of the specification of the economic objectives of statutory financial regulation by the FSA. Llewellyn (1999) used authoritative and coherent language when discussing the economic case for regulation, although Llewellyn does not make a clear case for statutory regulation of securities markets transactions. When the FSA itself makes cases for or against regulation, rather than use economic language, it hides behind general phrases that could justify any amount of intervention: 'maintaining public confidence', 'providing consumer protection', 'preventing market abuse', etc. This should not be surprising as these phrases lie at the heart of the FSA's objectives as laid down by FSMA 2000. It is rare for any consideration to be given by the FSA to whether these objectives are best achieved by statutory regulation or by private regulation and competition. It is even rarer for the economic rationale for the pursuit, by a statutory regulator, of those particular objectives to be considered. This compares unfavourably both with the Bank of England's and Ofcom's efforts to provide a rigorous underpinning for their interventions.[3]

This state of affairs is not the fault of the FSA – at least not necessarily so. First, the FSA is echoing the principles laid down by the FSMA 2000 and it is only natural for it to do that: indeed, it is its legal duty. Second, because of its history the FSA is a strange mix of an evolved private regulator (albeit one that has been monopolised and effectively nationalised) and a state regulator. It is therefore only natural that some of its functions are not the normal and limited functions that economists believe should be given to statutory regulators. The argument here is not that such functions (maintaining market confidence, market efficiency, and so on) do not need performing, but that they should be performed through regulatory structures that evolve through the market itself.

A return to evolution

The return to private institutions of the role of rule-making for investment transactions is not proposed as a 'problem-free' solution to investment market regulation. There will be issues that

---

3   Whether we agree with the Bank of England's or Ofcom's analysis is beside the point.

have to be dealt with, some by the criminal or civil law, some by exchanges themselves, perhaps some by the competition authorities and possibly some by special laws passed by Parliament for a specific purpose. Surely, however, the burden of proof should be on those who want to undermine freedom and impose government regulation on private transactions.

There is little comparative data on the relative merits of state and private regulation of stock market transactions because of the way that regulation by the state has taken over around the world. As such, much of our approach has been deductive rather than empirical. Nevertheless, the limited studies that there have been point strongly in the direction of private regulation. Romano (1998), writing about a slightly different proposal of decentralisation of regulatory responsibility to the US states, produces ample evidence to suggest that statutory regulation of investment markets is not necessary. For example, she quotes George Benston, who found that before the enactment of US Federal Securities laws in the 1930s, companies voluntarily provided all relevant information to investors except – in some cases – that about sales. Furthermore, the enhanced mandated disclosure of sales information made no difference to share prices. Companies need funds, argues Romano; it is therefore not surprising that they will provide their owners with information without being told to do so. Furthermore, according to Romano, non-UK companies listing in London generally comply with the enhanced disclosure requirements of the London market even if they do not have to do so under EU rules. Romano also argues that mandatory accounting standards required by statutory regulators do not lead to more important information being made available to investors.

We also have evidence from the UK and abroad from an

analysis of the history of exchanges that suggests that stock exchanges can and did do the things now done by government regulators. Furthermore, they did them very effectively. Again, the burden of proof must surely fall on those who believe in statutory regulation to demonstrate that it is more effective. The burden of proof should be high because of the danger that state regulation can crowd out new, unforeseeable, regulatory innovations and because of the ability of state regulators to pursue objectives that are contrary to the interests of market participants, as predicted by public choice economics. Romano summarises the position in the most succinct way possible, and we cannot improve on her conclusion: companies will not list on exchanges that have the lowest regulatory requirements but on the exchange that has the system of rules that leads to the lowest cost of capital. This is the soundest argument possible for competing exchanges and a process of competition between private regulators so that we can continually discover better sets of rules.

The positive arguments for private regulation are strengthened when the arguments against state regulation are considered. Whatever may be the shortcomings of a market economy, the public choice arguments against state regulation are compelling. If we accept state regulation of investment markets we are assuming that a regulatory bureau accountable to a department of government disciplined by a quinquennial election can correct whatever failings there may be in market-based regulation. This is a strong assumption and one that is crucially undermined by public choice economics. The behaviour and outcomes of financial regulation by the state in the UK seem to be exactly those predicted by public choice economics: incessant rule-writing, increasing costs, a 'something must be done' response to crises, corporate capture, the pursuit of the interests of regulators themselves and a lack of focus (exacerbated in the UK by the FSA's statutory objectives).

Furthermore, the FSA is one institution among many in the UK which has powers that go beyond the rule of law. Over the last generation, we have become used to 'enabling legislation', which gives ministers powers to write new regulations that are not debated in the House of Commons. The FSA and other similar bodies take this one step farther. The FSA is allowed to write rules with no direct accountability at all – either to the market or to the elected government. As we have seen, its enforcement powers are questionable too if we accept the normal principles of the rule of law. Indeed, the argument of F. A. Hayek in *The Constitution of Liberty* will probably resonate with many people reading this monograph whose area of specialisation is not the financial sector, so pervasive is the problem of discretionary administrative power: the 'power of the professional administrator ... is now the main threat to individual liberty' (Hayek, 1960: 202).

It seems that the recent crisis has been followed by a rush of prosecutions, fines and crusades against bonuses – together with more regulations. Populism is the order of the day.

We have shown decisively that such discretionary power is not necessary. Practical arguments in favour of statutory financial regulation need to be very strong. We have uncovered no evidence to convince us that there are such strong arguments in the UK. As such, we propose that we return investment market regulation to market institutions, remove or disperse other functions of the FSA, and wind the body up.

Is there a pragmatic way forward?

The purpose of IEA monographs is to point out the virtues of a different paradigm of thinking from that prevailing in political and intellectual circles. Our proposals are not impractical given the recent history of UK financial markets. We have recently had self-governing stock exchanges. It is difficult, however, to imagine a government implementing our proposals rapidly. Might there be an indirect way to proceed?

There is no point proposing that the FSA restructures or reduces regulatory interference. We have no view on whether the FSA might or might not do its job better if it did so. It is simply the wrong model to generate appropriate rules and regulations. If there is to be step-by-step reform, then perhaps the following routes could be followed.

First, regional stock exchanges should be allowed to develop on which firms raise capital and shares are traded up to a certain market capitalisation. These stock exchanges should be entirely exempt from all financial regulation – except general law. The companies should also be exempt from all accounting and reporting standards – these would be determined by exchanges. Indeed, the new coalition government might take note of the Liberal Democrat manifesto for the 2010 election:[4] 'We will ... support the establishment of ... Regional Stock Exchanges. Regional Stock Exchanges will be a route for businesses to access equity without the heavy regulatory requirements of a London listing.' Such exchanges should be exempt from all other regulation – including that arising from the FSA – too. They should be trusted to develop their own rules and governance systems.

4   See: http://www.libdems.org.uk/our_manifesto.aspx.

Unfortunately, there was no mention of this proposal in the coalition agreement when the Conservative/Liberal Democrat government was formed.[5]

Second, following this model, the Alternative Investment Market (AIM) should be allowed to establish a sub-market where companies that are quoted only on AIM and no other exchange could be traded according to rules developed by the exchange itself with no interference from the FSA.

These are clearly small concessions – and they are inadequate given the challenges we face from discretionary regulation by administrative bodies. But if they are seen to work, they will provide pressure for a more general return of regulation to the market along the lines we have proposed in this monograph.

5   See: http://www.libdems.org.uk/latest_news_detail.aspx?title=Conservative_
    Liberal_Democrat_coalition_agreements&pPK=2697bcdc-7483–47a7-a517–
    7778979458ff.

REFERENCES

Akerlof, G. A. (1970), 'The market for "lemons": quality, uncertainty and the market mechanism', *Quarterly Journal of Economics*, 84(3): 488–500.

Alcock, A. (2000), *The Financial Services and Markets Act 2000: A Guide to the New Law*, UK: Jordans.

Arthur T. G. and P. M. Booth (2006), 'Financial regulation, the state and the market: is the Financial Services Authority an unnecessary evil?', *Economic Affairs*, 26(2): 22–30.

Beny, L. (2001), *US Secondary Stock Markets: A Survey of Current Regulatory and Structural Issues and a Reform Proposal to Enhance Competition*, Cambridge, MA: Centre for Law, Economics and Business, Harvard Law School.

Better Regulation Task Force (2003), *Imaginative Thinking for Better Regulation*, London: Better Regulation Task Force.

Bishops' Conference of England and Wales (2010), *Choosing the Common Good*, Stoke on Trent: Bishops' Conference.

Blundell, J. and C. Robinson (eds) (2000), *Regulation without the State ... The Debate Continues*, Readings 52, London: Institute of Economic Affairs.

Boehmer, B. and E. Boehmer (2002), *Trading Your Neighbor's EFT: Competition or Fragmentation?*, Capital Markets Institute

Conference, Toronto, August, www.rotman.utoronto.ca/
cmi/news/boehmer.pdf.

Booth, P. M. (2003), 'Competition in financial regulation', in P.
M. Booth and D. A. Currie (eds), *The Regulation of Financial
Markets*, Readings 58, London: Institute of Economic Affairs.

Booth P. M. (2007), '"Freedom with publicity" – the actuarial
profession and insurance regulation from 1844–1945', *Annals
of Actuarial Science*, 2(1): 115–46.

Booth, P. M. (ed.) (2009), *Verdict on the Crash: Causes and Policy
Implications*, Hobart Paperback 37, London: Institute of
Economic Affairs.

Boyfield, K. (2006), *Selling the City Short? A Review of the EU's
Financial Services Action Plan*, London: Open Union in
association with Keith Boyfield Associates.

Burns, J. (1909), *Stock Exchange Investments in Theory and Practice*,
London: Charles and Edwin Layton (for the Institute of
Actuaries).

Byrne, A., D. Harrison, B. Rhodes and D. Blake (2006), 'Pyrrhic
victory? The unintended consequence of the Pensions Act
2004', *Economic Affairs*, 26(3): 9–16.

CESR (2003), 'Preparing for implementation of International
Financial Reporting Standards (IFRS)', press release 14–03,
Committee of European Securities Regulators.

Chittenden, F., H. Foster and B. Sloan (2010), *Taxation and Red
Tape: The Cost to British Business of Complying with the UK
Tax System*, Research Monograph 64, London: Institute of
Economic Affairs.

City of London (2009), *Assessing the Effectiveness of Enforcement
and Regulation*, London: City of London Corporation.

Coase, R. H. (1960), 'The problem of social cost', *Journal of Law and Economics*, 3: 1–44.

Coase, R. H. (1974), 'The lighthouse in economics', *Journal of Law and Economics*, 17(2): 357–76.

Congdon, T. (2003), 'The goal of a single European financial market', in P. M. and D. A. Currie (eds), *The Regulation of Financial Markets*, Readings 58, London: Institute of Economic Affairs.

Congdon, T. (2008), *Northern Rock and the European Union*, London: Global Vision.

Congdon, T. (2009), *Central Banking in a Free Society*, Hobart Paper 166, London: Institute of Economic Affairs, http://www.iea.org.uk/record.jsp?type=book&ID=450.

Conservative Party (2009), *From Crisis to Confidence: Plan for Sound Banking*, policy paper, London: Conservative Party.

Crockett, A., T. Harris, F. S. Mishkin and E. N. White (2003), *Conflicts of Interest in the Financial Services Industry: What Should We Do about Them*, London: Centre for Economic Policy Research.

Davies, H. (2002), *Rethinking the Listing Regime*, Speech to the Annual Listing Rules Conference, London.

Davis, E. P. and B. Steil (2001), *Institutional Investors*, Cambridge, MA: MIT Press.

Daykin, C. D. (2004), 'Trust and professional responsibility in a liberal market', *Economic Affairs*, 24(2): 11–18.

Easterbrook, F. H. (1981), 'Insider trading, secret agents, evidentiary privileges, and the production of information', *Supreme Court Review*, pp. 309–65.

Europe Economics (2003), *The Cost of Regulation Study*, London: Europe Economics.

FSA (2000), *Market Abuse: A Draft Code of Market Conduct*, London: Financial Services Authority.

FSA (2001), *The FSA's Approach to Regulation of Market Infrastructure*, Feedback Statement, London: Financial Services Authority.

FSA (2002), *Investment Research: Conflicts and Other Issues*, Discussion Paper 15, London: Financial Services Authority.

FSA (2003), *Reasonable Expectations: Regulation in a non-zero failure world*, London: Financial Services Authority.

FSA (2004), *The Listing Review and Implementation of the Prospectus Directive* (Draft rules and feedback on CP203), London: Financial Services Authority.

FSA (2005a), *International Regulatory Outlook*, London: Financial Services Authority.

FSA (2005b), *Financial Risk Outlook*, London: Financial Services Authority.

FSA (2006), *A Guide to Market Failure and High Level Cost Benefit Analysis*, London: Financial Services Authority.

Galbraith, J. K. (1955), *The Great Crash 1929*, Boston, MA, and New York: Houghton Mifflin.

Grant, R. W. (1999), *The Incredible Bread Machine: A Study of Capitalism, Freedom, and the State*, 2nd edn, San Francisco, CA: Fox & Wilkes.

Hayek, F. A. (1960), *The Constitution of Liberty*, London: Routledge and Kegan Paul.

HM Treasury and FSA (2004), *UK Implementation of the Prospectus Directive 2003/71/EC*, London: HMSO.

HM Treasury, Bank of England and FSA (2003), 'The EU Financial Services Action Plan: a guide', reprinted in *Bank of England Quarterly Bulletin*, 43(3): 352–65.

Ho, R. Y., R. Strange and J. Piesse (2004), *Institutional Features of the Hong Kong Stock Market: Implications for Asset Pricing*, Research Paper 027, Management Centre Research Papers, London: King's College.

Klein, D. (2000), *Assurance and Trust in a Great Society*, Irvington-on-Hudson, New York: Foundation for Economic Education, Inc.

Kynaston, D. (2002), *The City of London, vol. IV: A Club No More, 1945–2006*, London: Pimlico.

La Porta, R., F. Lopez de Silanes and A. Shleifer (2006), 'What works in securities laws?', *Journal of Finance*, 61(1): 1–32.

Lightfoot, W. (2003), 'Managing financial crises', in P. M. Booth and D. A. Currie (eds), *The Regulation of Financial Markets*, Readings 58, London: Institute of Economic Affairs.

Llewellyn, D. (1999), *The Economic Rationale for Financial Regulation*, Occasional Paper 1, London: Financial Services Authority.

London Stock Exchange (2006), *Understanding MiFID*, London: London Stock Exchange.

London Stock Exchange/Oxera (2006), *The Cost of Capital: An International Comparison*, London: City of London.

Macey, J. and M. O'Hara (2005), 'From orders to markets', *Regulation*, Summer, pp. 62–70.

Mahoney, P. (1997), 'The exchange as regulator', *Virginia Law Review*, 83(7): 1453–500.

Michie, R. (1999), *The London Stock Exchange: A History*, Oxford: Oxford University Press.

Morgan Stanley and Mercer Oliver Wyman (2003), *Structural Shifts in Securities Trading: Outlook for European Exchanges*,

http://www.mow.com/en/perspectives/documents/
StructuralShiftsinSecuritiesTrading-MOWJun03.pdf.

Morrison, A. D. (2004), 'Life insurance: regulation as contract enforcement', *Economic Affairs*, 24(4): 47–52.

Myddelton, D. R. (2004), *Unshackling Accountants*, Hobart Paper 149, London: Institute of Economic Affairs.

Norberg, J. (2009), *Financial Fiasco: How America's Infatuation with Home Ownership and Easy Money Created the Economic Crisis*, Washington, DC: Cato Institute.

Oesterle, D. A. (2000), *Securities Markets Regulation: Time to Move to a Market-based Approach*, Policy Analysis no. 374, Washington, DC: Cato Institute.

Padilla, A. (2002), 'Can agency theory justify the regulation of insider trading?', *Quarterly Journal of Austrian Economics*, 5(1): 3–38.

Pritchard, A. (2003), 'Self-regulation and securities markets', *Regulation*, Spring, pp. 32–9.

Richards, E., R. Foster and T. Kiedrowski (2006), *Communications – the next decade: A collection of essays prepared for the UK Office of Communications*, London: Ofcom.

Romano, R. (1998), 'Empowering investors: a market approach to securities regulation', Yale School of Management Working Papers no. 74, http://ideas.repec.org/p/ysm/somwrk/ysm74.html.

Romano, R. (2005), 'The Sarbanes-Oxley Act and the making of quack corporate governance', *Yale Law Journal*, 114(7): 1585–91.

Rothbard, M. (1983), *America's Great Depression*, 4th edn, New York: Richardson and Snyder.

Rothbard, M. (1995), *Making Economic Sense*, Auburn, AL: Ludwig von Mises Institute.

Sternberg, E. (2004), *Corporate Governance: Accountability in the Marketplace*, Hobart Paper 147, London: Institute of Economic Affairs.

Stringham, E. (2002) 'The emergence of the London Stock Exchange as a self-policing club', *Journal of Private Enterprise*, 17(2): 1–19.

Stringham, E. (2003), 'The extra-legal development of securities trading in seventeenth century Amsterdam', *Quarterly Review of Economics and Finance*, 43(2): 321–44.

Stringham, E. and P. J. Boettke (2004), 'Brokers, bureaucrats and the emergence of financial markets, *Managerial Finance*, 30(5): 57–71.

Stringham, E. and P. J. Boettke (2006), 'The failings of legal centralism for helping stock markets in transition', *Politicka Ekonomie*, 1: 21–33.

Tullock, G., A. Seldon and G. L. Brady (2000), *Government: Whose Obedient Servant?*, IEA Readings 51, London: Institute of Economic Affairs.

Turner, Lord (2009), *The Turner Review: A regulatory response to the global banking crisis*, London: FSA.

ABOUT THE IEA

The Institute is a research and educational charity (No. CC 235 351), limited by guarantee. Its mission is to improve understanding of the fundamental institutions of a free society by analysing and expounding the role of markets in solving economic and social problems.

The IEA achieves its mission by:

- a high-quality publishing programme
- conferences, seminars, lectures and other events
- outreach to school and college students
- brokering media introductions and appearances

The IEA, which was established in 1955 by the late Sir Antony Fisher, is an educational charity, not a political organisation. It is independent of any political party or group and does not carry on activities intended to affect support for any political party or candidate in any election or referendum, or at any other time. It is financed by sales of publications, conference fees and voluntary donations.

In addition to its main series of publications the IEA also publishes a quarterly journal, *Economic Affairs*.

The IEA is aided in its work by a distinguished international Academic Advisory Council and an eminent panel of Honorary Fellows. Together with other academics, they review prospective IEA publications, their comments being passed on anonymously to authors. All IEA papers are therefore subject to the same rigorous independent refereeing process as used by leading academic journals.

IEA publications enjoy widespread classroom use and course adoptions in schools and universities. They are also sold throughout the world and often translated/reprinted.

Since 1974 the IEA has helped to create a worldwide network of 100 similar institutions in over 70 countries. They are all independent but share the IEA's mission.

Views expressed in the IEA's publications are those of the authors, not those of the Institute (which has no corporate view), its Managing Trustees, Academic Advisory Council members or senior staff.

Members of the Institute's Academic Advisory Council, Honorary Fellows, Trustees and Staff are listed on the following page.

The Institute gratefully acknowledges financial support for its publications programme and other work from a generous benefaction by the late Alec and Beryl Warren.

The Institute of Economic Affairs
2 Lord North Street, Westminster, London SW1P 3LB
Tel: 020 7799 8900
Fax: 020 7799 2137
Email: iea@iea.org.uk
Internet: iea.org.uk

Other papers recently published by the IEA include:

A Market in Airport Slots
Keith Boyfield (editor), David Starkie, Tom Bass & Barry Humphreys
Readings 56; ISBN 0 255 36505 5; £10.00

Money, Inflation and the Constitutional Position of the Central Bank
Milton Friedman & Charles A. E. Goodhart
Readings 57; ISBN 0 255 36538 1; £10.00

railway.com
Parallels between the Early British Railways and the ICT Revolution
Robert C. B. Miller
Research Monograph 57; ISBN 0 255 36534 9; £12.50

The Regulation of Financial Markets
Edited by Philip Booth & David Currie
Readings 58; ISBN 0 255 36551 9; £12.50

Climate Alarmism Reconsidered
Robert L. Bradley Jr
Hobart Paper 146; ISBN 0 255 36541 1; £12.50

Government Failure: E. G. West on Education
Edited by James Tooley & James Stanfield
Occasional Paper 130; ISBN 0 255 36552 7; £12.50

Corporate Governance: Accountability in the Marketplace
Elaine Sternberg
Second edition
Hobart Paper 147; ISBN 0 255 36542 x; £12.50

The Land Use Planning System
Evaluating Options for Reform
John Corkindale
Hobart Paper 148; ISBN 0 255 36550 0; £10.00

Economy and Virtue
Essays on the Theme of Markets and Morality
Edited by Dennis O'Keeffe
Readings 59; ISBN 0 255 36504 7; £12.50

Free Markets Under Siege
Cartels, Politics and Social Welfare
Richard A. Epstein
Occasional Paper 132; ISBN 0 255 36553 5; £10.00

Unshackling Accountants
D. R. Myddelton
Hobart Paper 149; ISBN 0 255 36559 4; £12.50

The Euro as Politics
Pedro Schwartz
Research Monograph 58; ISBN 0 255 36535 7; £12.50

Pricing Our Roads
Vision and Reality
Stephen Glaister & Daniel J. Graham
Research Monograph 59; ISBN 0 255 36562 4; £10.00

The Role of Business in the Modern World
Progress, Pressures, and Prospects for the Market Economy
David Henderson
Hobart Paper 150; ISBN 0 255 36548 9; £12.50

Public Service Broadcasting Without the BBC?
Alan Peacock
Occasional Paper 133; ISBN 0 255 36565 9; £10.00

The ECB and the Euro: the First Five Years
Otmar Issing
Occasional Paper 134; ISBN 0 255 36555 1; £10.00

Towards a Liberal Utopia?
Edited by Philip Booth
Hobart Paperback 32; ISBN 0 255 36563 2; £15.00

The Way Out of the Pensions Quagmire
Philip Booth & Deborah Cooper
Research Monograph 60; ISBN 0 255 36517 9; £12.50

Black Wednesday
A Re-examination of Britain's Experience in the Exchange Rate Mechanism
Alan Budd
Occasional Paper 135; ISBN 0 255 36566 7; £7.50

Crime: Economic Incentives and Social Networks
Paul Ormerod
Hobart Paper 151; ISBN 0 255 36554 3; £10.00

The Road to Serfdom *with* **The Intellectuals and Socialism**
Friedrich A. Hayek
Occasional Paper 136; ISBN 0 255 36576 4; £10.00

Money and Asset Prices in Boom and Bust
Tim Congdon
Hobart Paper 152; ISBN 0 255 36570 5; £10.00

The Dangers of Bus Re-regulation
and Other Perspectives on Markets in Transport
John Hibbs et al.
Occasional Paper 137; ISBN 0 255 36572 1; £10.00

The New Rural Economy
Change, Dynamism and Government Policy
Berkeley Hill et al.
Occasional Paper 138; ISBN 0 255 36546 2; £15.00

The Benefits of Tax Competition
Richard Teather
Hobart Paper 153; ISBN 0 255 36569 1; £12.50

Wheels of Fortune
Self-funding Infrastructure and the Free Market Case for a Land Tax
Fred Harrison
Hobart Paper 154; ISBN 0 255 36589 6; £12.50

Were 364 Economists All Wrong?
Edited by Philip Booth
Readings 60; ISBN 978 0 255 36588 8; £10.00

Europe After the 'No' Votes
Mapping a New Economic Path
Patrick A. Messerlin
Occasional Paper 139; ISBN 978 0 255 36580 2; £10.00

The Railways, the Market and the Government
John Hibbs et al.
Readings 61; ISBN 978 0 255 36567 3; £12.50

Corruption: The World's Big C
Cases, Causes, Consequences, Cures
Ian Senior
Research Monograph 61; ISBN 978 0 255 36571 0; £12.50

Choice and the End of Social Housing
Peter King
Hobart Paper 155; ISBN 978 0 255 36568 0; £10.00

Sir Humphrey's Legacy
Facing Up to the Cost of Public Sector Pensions
Neil Record
Hobart Paper 156; ISBN 978 0 255 36578 9; £10.00

The Economics of Law
Cento Veljanovski
Second edition
Hobart Paper 157; ISBN 978 0 255 36561 1; £12.50

Living with Leviathan
Public Spending, Taxes and Economic Performance
David B. Smith
Hobart Paper 158; ISBN 978 0 255 36579 6; £12.50

The Vote Motive
Gordon Tullock
New edition
Hobart Paperback 33; ISBN 978 0 255 36577 2; £10.00

Waging the War of Ideas
John Blundell
Third edition
Occasional Paper 131; ISBN 978 0 255 36606 9; £12.50

The War Between the State and the Family
How Government Divides and Impoverishes
Patricia Morgan
Hobart Paper 159; ISBN 978 0 255 36596 3; £10.00

Capitalism – A Condensed Version
Arthur Seldon
Occasional Paper 140; ISBN 978 0 255 36598 7; £7.50

Catholic Social Teaching and the Market Economy
Edited by Philip Booth
Hobart Paperback 34; ISBN 978 0 255 36581 9; £15.00

Adam Smith – A Primer
Eamonn Butler
Occasional Paper 141; ISBN 978 0 255 36608 3; £7.50

Happiness, Economics and Public Policy
Helen Johns & Paul Ormerod
Research Monograph 62; ISBN 978 0 255 36600 7; £10.00

They Meant Well
Government Project Disasters
D. R. Myddelton
Hobart Paper 160; ISBN 978 0 255 36601 4; £12.50

Rescuing Social Capital from Social Democracy
John Meadowcroft & Mark Pennington
Hobart Paper 161; ISBN 978 0 255 36592 5; £10.00

Paths to Property
Approaches to Institutional Change in International Development
Karol Boudreaux & Paul Dragos Aligica
Hobart Paper 162; ISBN 978 0 255 36582 6; £10.00

Prohibitions
Edited by John Meadowcroft
Hobart Paperback 35; ISBN 978 0 255 36585 7; £15.00

Trade Policy, New Century
The WTO, FTAs and Asia Rising
Razeen Sally
Hobart Paper 163; ISBN 978 0 255 36544 4; £12.50

Sixty Years On – Who Cares for the NHS?
Helen Evans
Research Monograph 63; ISBN 978 0 255 36611 3; £10.00

Taming Leviathan
Waging the War of Ideas Around the World
Edited by Colleen Dyble
Occasional Paper 142; ISBN 978 0 255 36607 6; £12.50

The Legal Foundations of Free Markets
Edited by Stephen F. Copp
Hobart Paperback 36; ISBN 978 0 255 36591 8; £15.00

Ludwig von Mises – A Primer
Eamonn Butler
Occasional Paper 143; ISBN 978 0 255 36629 8; £7.50

Other IEA publications

Comprehensive information on other publications and the wider work of the IEA can be found at www.iea.org.uk. To order any publication please see below.

Personal customers

Orders from personal customers should be directed to the IEA:
Bob Layson
IEA
2 Lord North Street
FREEPOST LON10168
London SW1P 3YZ
Tel: 020 7799 8909. Fax: 020 7799 2137
Email: blayson@iea.org.uk

Trade customers

All orders from the book trade should be directed to the IEA's distributor:
Gazelle Book Services Ltd (IEA Orders)
FREEPOST RLYS-EAHU-YSCZ
White Cross Mills
Hightown
Lancaster LA1 4XS
Tel: 01524 68765, Fax: 01524 53232
Email: sales@gazellebooks.co.uk

IEA subscriptions

The IEA also offers a subscription service to its publications. For a single annual payment (currently £42.00 in the UK), subscribers receive every monograph the IEA publishes. For more information please contact:
Adam Myers
Subscriptions
IEA
2 Lord North Street
FREEPOST LON10168
London SW1P 3YZ
Tel: 020 7799 8920, Fax: 020 7799 2137
Email: amyers@iea.org.uk